Bedside Companion for Gardeners

Bedside Companion for Gardeners

An anthology of garden writing for every night of the year

EDITED BY JANE MCMORLAND HUNTER

BATSFORD

First published in the United Kingdom in 2021 by
B.T. Batsford
43 Great Ormond Street
London WC1N 3HZ

An imprint of B.T. Batsford Holdings Ltd

ISBN: 9781849947138

A CIP catalogue record for this book is available from the
British Library.

10 9 8 7 6 5 4 3 2

Reproduction by Rival Colour Ltd, UK
Printed by Bell & Bain Ltd, UK

This book can be ordered direct from the publisher
at www.batsford.com

Illustrations by Kristen Knechtel

CONTENTS

To Sue and David, gardeners and readers,
and obviously to Matilda,
with all my love.

Acknowledgements

As always, a huge thank you to everyone at Hatchards for
looking after my books so well and coming up with so many
helpful suggestions. Friends have scoured their shelves for me,
in particular Sue and David Gibb, Louy and David Piachaud, Ian
Prince, Francis Cleverdon and Julie Apps. My editors at Batsford,
Tina Persaud and Lilly Phelan, make compiling these anthologies
a pleasure and Teresa Chris provides invaluable agency support. To
quote so many other writers: everything would get done faster but
less pleasurably without Matilda's presence.

About the editor

Jane McMorland Hunter has compiled nine anthologies for
Batsford and the National Trust including collections on nature,
friendship, London, England and the First World War. She has
also worked as a gardener, potter and quilter, writes gardening,
cookery and craft books, and works at Hatchards Bookshop in
Piccadilly. Brought up in the country, she now lives in London
where she has a house full of gardening (and other) books and a
small but much-loved garden.

Introduction

Of the many anthologies I have compiled, this one is definitely the closest to my heart. Much of my adult life has been spent working in gardens, pottering in them or sitting in them, either reading or simply appreciating the outside space. Even when I didn't have a garden I had window boxes and spent much of my spare time reading about gardens and making plans for when I finally had one of my own. Mirabel Osler wrote in her book *A Gentle Plea for Chaos* that one doesn't need to garden to garden. I would take the idea one step further and say that one doesn't even need a garden to garden: you can visit gardens, peer over walls and round fences, make plans for gardens you might have one day and read about them. The aim of this anthology is to satisfy the last of those activities.

Pieces of poetry and prose, fact and fiction, practical advice and wildly impractical ideas are collected together here, with one piece for every night of the year. My intention was that there would be a balance of the different elements but I hunted down the pieces I liked with no real plan. The result was far too much Dickens, too many pieces about mulberries and cottage garden flowers and vast sections from Frances Hodgson Burnett's *The Secret Garden*. A few wild flowers have also crept in but most of these would happily grace any garden given the opportunity. I did a little pruning but decided that most pieces should stay. As a result the anthology is a little like a slightly unruly climbing rose, tethered to its framework and following a proscribed outline but every so often shooting off at a wild tangent.

The gardening pieces and anything containing practical advice have been put into the appropriate seasons but I have taken liberties with fiction, poetry and children's stories, reasoning that magic beans could grow at any time of year and seasons on the moon might not necessarily align with ours on earth. Some pieces follow on from each other while others take the reader off in a new direction. Most are fairly short, my aim being that they will create a picture, inspire a thought or offer a brief horticultural insight of some kind. Many do not even refer to gardening directly, the garden being a backdrop against which the action takes place. But even that is enough, just as a glimpse through the gap in a hedge is enough to set our imaginations working.

This is not intended to be a practical manual. Each month I have included practical advice from John Evelyn in 1664, Samuel Orchart Beeton (husband of Isabella) from two hundred years later and others from the sixteenth to the twentieth centuries. Some show how little gardening has changed whilst others seem to have been written with another world in mind. Each extract is dated and I would recommend that readers check when the piece was written before rushing into the garden to put the idea into practice.

Many of these pieces are set in time, which is why I have given the date the original book was written or first published and the author's dates. Styles and opinions in both gardening and literature change over the years, often dramatically. The Romans took a practical approach to gardening but, during the unsettled times of the Middle Ages, gardens in literature were frequently used as a backdrop for lovelorn suitors. As life became more settled, gardening became a practical and useful option for more people and manuals began to appear. One of the first, by Thomas Tusser, was written in verse as he felt the working man would understand and remember poetry better than prose. In the late eighteenth century professional designers began to play an important role in the gardens of the rich. William Kent, Lancelot 'Capability' Brown and others were loved and hated in equal measure, arousing passionate feelings and prompting novelists such as Jane Austen and Thomas Love Peacock to poke fun at their 'improvements'. From then on, everyone had an opinion about everything. Old-fashioned flowers were charming or outdated, fountains esteemed or unwholesome and some grottos fit only for toads. Shrubberies, temples and topiary have all, at various stages, been in or out of fashion. Some writers intend to be amusing, notably Heath Robinson on poets and Karel Čapek on the dangers involved in watering, whilst others have become humorous as time advances and tastes change. I have tried, but not very hard, to be fair to all sides.

Nearly all these pieces are extracts from larger works. They may not necessarily be particularly representative of the author but the fact that I liked them was enough. In almost all cases there were other extracts I wanted to include but my choices were curbed by space and copyright constraints. At times I felt like George E. Ohr, otherwise known as the Mad Potter of Biloxi, who, when asked to send a sample of his work replied: 'I send you four pieces, but it is as easy to pass judgement on my productions from four pieces as it would be to take four lines from Shakespeare and guess the rest.' In each case the original source is given for readers who wish to read more.

Gardening can be a source of great pleasure, whether one is planning, planting and pruning or simply escaping from the busy world beyond the garden gate. Just as importantly, reading about gardens can be a source of delight and inspiration. My hope is that everyone will find pieces to delight and inspire them in this collection: some old friends and other welcome new discoveries.

Not wholly in the busy world, nor quite
Beyond it, blooms the garden that I love.

From *The Gardener's Daughter* | Alfred, Lord Tennyson

JANUARY

An Earthly Paradise

Monochrome

From *The Morville Hours*, 2008 | Katherine Swift (1956–)

I still love the garden best in monochrome: in snow, in
moonlight, in frost, in heavy dew, in fog – especially in freezing
fog, when whole trees are drowned fathoms deep in arctic air
and the boundaries between sky and ground blur, when the
silvered paths of the garden seem to float over the black earth
of the empty beds like slender bridges cantilevered out over
a chasm, and twigs and branches are transformed by the hoar
frost into fragile constructions of air and ice, each day a little
longer, growing in the direction in which the air is flowing, like
fingerposts to the far north.

1 January

Wilderness

From *Great Expectations, 1860–1861* | Charles Dickens (1812–1870)

I strolled into the garden, and strolled all over it. It was quite
a wilderness, and there were old melon-frames and cucumber-
frames in it, which seemed in their decline to have produced a
spontaneous growth of weak attempts at pieces of old hats and
boots, with now and then a weedy offshoot into the likeness of a
battered saucepan.

Not a Quite Dead Garden

From *The Secret Garden, 1911* | Frances Hodgson Burnett (1849–1924)

'I wonder if they are all quite dead,' she said. 'Is it all a quite dead garden? I wish it wasn't.'

If she had been Ben Weatherstaff she could have told whether the wood was alive by looking at it, but she could only see that there were only grey or brown sprays and branches and none showed any signs of even a tiny leaf-bud anywhere.

. . . .

She thought she saw something sticking out of the black earth – some sharp little pale green points. She remembered what Ben Weatherstaff had said and she knelt down to look at them.

'Yes, they are tiny growing things and they might be crocuses or snowdrops or daffodils,' she whispered.

She bent very close to them and sniffed the fresh scent of the damp earth. She liked it very much.

'Perhaps there are some other ones coming up in other places,' she said. 'I will go all over the garden and look.'

She did not skip, but walked. She went slowly and kept her eyes on the ground. She looked in the old border-beds and among the grass, and after she had gone round, trying to miss nothing, she had found ever so many more sharp, pale green points, and she had become quite excited again.

'It isn't a quite dead garden,' she cried out softly to herself.

More Orchards and Gardens

From *The Country Housewifes Garden, 1618* | William Lawson
(c.1554–1635)

A Garden requireth not so large a scope of ground as an Orchard both in regard of the much weeding, dressing and removing, and also the pains in a Garden is not so well repayed home, as in an Orchard: It is to be granted, that the Kitchen garden doth yeeld rich grains, by berries, roots, cabbages &c. yet these are no way comparable to the fruits of a rich Orchard: But notwithstanding I am of opinion, that it were better for *England* that we had more Orchards and Gardens, and more large. And therefore we leave the quantity to every mans ability and will.

The Enchanted Garden

E. Nesbit (1858–1924)

Oh, what a garden it was, living gold, living green,
Full of enchantments like spices embalming the air,
There, where you fled and I followed – you ever unseen,
Yet each glad pulse of me cried to my heart, 'She is there!'

Roses and lilies and lilies and roses again,
Tangle of leaves and white magic of blossoming trees,
Sunlight that lay where, last moment, your footstep had lain –
Was not the garden enchanted that proffered me these?

Ah, what a garden it is since I caught you at last –
Scattered the magic and shattered the spell with a kiss:
Wintry and dreary and cold with the wind of the past,
Ah that a garden enchanted should wither to this!

The First Garden

From *Genesis 2: 8–10* | The King James Bible, 1611

And the Lord God planted a garden eastward in Eden; and there he put the man whom he had formed.

And out of the ground made the Lord God to grow every tree that is pleasant to the sight, and good for food; the tree of life also in the midst of the garden, and the tree of knowledge of good and evil.

And a river went out of Eden to water the garden.

6 January

The Parson's Garden

From *In a Gloucestershire Garden, 1895* | Rev. Henry N. Ellacombe
(1822–1916)

I would only say generally, that the love of flowers and gardening is so universal amongst the English peasantry that a country parson will often find a better introduction to a cottager through his garden than by any other means. And though the love of flowers is so universal, and the garden may be such a useful adjunct to the cottage, yet there is very great ignorance of the right principles of gardening, and the parson may be of great use to his poorer neighbours, not only by teaching, but still more by showing them better ways in his own garden. For the parsonage garden gate should be always open, and every parishioner welcomed; there need be no fear of any undue advantage being taken of the free permission to enter – the one difficulty will be to induce them to come in. And the parson may do much to brighten the gardens of his parish, and so to increase the interest in them by giving plants from his own garden.

Gardens for All Months

From *The Essays or Counsels, Civil and Moral: On Gardening, 1625* | Francis Bacon (1561–1626)

I do hold it, in the royal ordering of gardens, there ought to be gardens for all the months in the year; in which severally things of beauty may be then in season. For December, and January, and the latter part of November, you must take such things as are green all winter: holly; ivy; bays; juniper; cypress-trees; yew; pine-apple-trees; fir-trees; rosemary; lavender; periwinkle, the white, the purple, and the blue; germander; flags; orange-trees; lemon-trees; and myrtles, if they be stoved; and sweet marjoram, warm set. There followeth, for the latter part of January and February, the mezereon-tree, which then blossoms; crocus vernus, both the yellow and the grey; primroses; anemones; the early tulippa; hyacinthus orientalis; chamaïris; fritellaria.

. . . .

These particulars are for the climate of London; but my meaning is perceived, that you may have ver perpetuum, as the place affords.

Grand Plans for Thornton Lacey

From *Mansfield Park, 1814* | Jane Austen (1775–1817)

'The house must be turned to front the east instead of the north – the entrance and principal rooms I mean must be on that side where the view is really very pretty; I am sure it may be done. And *there* must be your approach – through what is at present the garden. You must make you a new garden at what is now the back of the house; which will be giving it the best aspect in the world – sloping to the south-east. The ground seems precisely formed for it. I rode fifty yards up the lane between the church and the house in order to look about me; and saw how it might all be. Nothing can be easier. The meadows beyond what *will be* the garden, as well as what now *is*, sweeping round from the lane I stood in to the north-east, that is, to the principal road through the village, must be all laid together of course; very pretty meadows they are, finely sprinkled with timber. They belong to the living, I suppose. If not, you must purchase them. Then the stream – something must be done with the stream; but I could not quite determine what. I had two or three ideas.'

The Winds

From *Five Hundred Points of Good Husbandry, 1557, 1573*

Thomas Tusser (1524–1580)

A description of the properties of windes at all times of the yeere

I North winds send haile, South winds bring raine,
East winds we bewail, West winds blow amaine:
North east is too cold, South east not too warme,
North west is too bold, South west doth no harme.

2 The north is a noyer to grasse of all suites,
The east a destroyer to herbe and all fruites:
The south with his showers refresheth the corne,
The west to all flowers may not be forborne.

3 The West, as a father, all goodnes doth bring,
The East, a forbearer, no manner of thing:
The South, as unkind, draweth sicknesse too neere,
The North, as a friend, maketh all againe cleere.

4 With temperate winde we be blessed of God,
With tempest we finde we are beat with his rod:
All power we knowe to remaine in his hand.
How ever winde blowe, by sea or by land.

Trimmed, Clothed, Disciplined

From *Old Country Life, 1890* | Rev. Sabine Baring-Gould (1834–1924)

Why should we imitate wild nature? The garden is a product of civilization. Why any more make of our gardens imitation wild nature, than paint our children with woad, and make them run about naked in an effort to make nature unadorned? The very charm of a garden is that it is taken out of savagery, trimmed, clothed, disciplined.

11 January

An Earthly Paradise

From *The Romance of the Rose c.1230, c.1275* | Guillaume de Lorris (c.1200–c.1240), Jean de Meun (c.1240–c.1305). Translated by F. S. Ellis (1830–1901)

LINES 645–680

No more I spake, but thanked kind fate,
When Idleness the garden gate
Threw open wide, and unafraid
To that sweet spot quick entry made.
Then burst on my astonished eyes
A dream – an Earthly Paradise:
And suddenly my soul seemed riven
From earth, to dwell in highest heaven;
Yet doubt I much if heaven can give
A place where I so soon would live
As this sweet garden, sacred haunt
Of birds whose soft melodious chaunt
Ravished mine ears; the nightingales
Here sang, and there the green wood-wales;
The bullfinch piped beneath, above,
I heard the crooning turtle-dove,
Near by, the sweet-voiced tiny wren,
While high in air, beyond my ken.
The skylark soared; the titmouse shrilled
The fauvette's gentle treble trilled,
The merle and mavis seemed to shake
The leaves in cadence, while each brake
With small fowl rang, as they would try
Their throats in choral rivalry.
'Twould seem as all and each of these
Sweet birds sang joyance to the breeze,

And then, their hearts disburdened, flew
To keep some loving rendezvous.
 The sweet melodious harmony
That winged its way from tree to tree.
With such soft symphony did fall
As concert 'twere celestial.
For never yet hath mortal ear
Been tuned such heavenlike songs to hear.
And past all thought it seemed that earth
Could give such glorious music birth.

The Garden in Faust

From *The Age of Innocence, 1920* | Edith Wharton (1862–1937)

THE OPERA HOUSE, NEW YORK:

The foreground, to the footlights, was covered with emerald green cloth. In the middle distance symmetrical mounds of woolly green moss bounded by croquet hoops formed the base of shrubs shaped like orange-trees but studded with large pink and red roses. Gigantic pansies, considerably larger than the roses, and closely resembling the floral pen-wipers made by female parishioners for fashionable clergymen, sprang from the moss beneath the rose-trees; and here and there a daisy grafted on a rose-branch flowered.

13 January

Finding the Right Book

From *Down the Garden Path, 1932* | Beverley Nichols (1898–1983)

It was during that first barren January that my passion for winter flowers developed into an obsession. I felt that somewhere somebody was waiting to tell me something. But who? And where? And what? I threw the catalogues into the fire, and watched their false pages curling into smoke. They were deceivers, those catalogues. I went back to London.

It was in such a state of depression that I strolled, one bleak January morning, into Messrs. Hatchard's bookshop at 187 Piccadilly. I was after a copy of George Moore's *Confessions of a Young Man*, for my own copy was almost worn out, so passionately had it been fondled. I walked into the shop, muttered something about 'looking for a book', and went to the shelves where Moore lay, in lofty seclusion.

But as I looked up, I saw that I had come to the wrong section. The books in front of me were all about gardening. They did not seem to be very attractive. They were mostly in wrappers which showed women in obsolete hats standing with guilty expressions

by the side of immense hollyhocks. They had terrible titles too
. . . like 'Romps in the Rockery' and 'A Garden of Memorie'. I
was about to pass on when suddenly I saw, right by my hand, a
book with a title that made me catch my breath in excitement.

It was called *Winter Blossoms from the Outdoor Garden*, by
A. W. Darnell.

Gingerly I stretched out my hand to take it. Would it vanish into
thin air? No. It was real enough. However, as I took it down, I
felt there must be some catch somewhere. For months I had been
vainly searching the catalogues and encyclopædias for even a few
paragraphs about winter flowers. And here was a whole book
devoted to the problem. Was the title a fake? Was it not a garden
book at all . . . was it perhaps an awful collection of short stories?
About thin sickly children who grew ivy in slums . . . and all that?

I opened it. As soon as I read the introduction my anxiety ceased.

A Bird Table

From *Gardening for the Ignorant, 1912* | Mrs Earle (1836–1925) and Ethel Case

An artistic-looking bird table is quite a pretty addition to a garden in winter, and feeding the birds keeps them from getting into the habit of attacking buds and blossoms, which have no food value, but are often pecked at and injured by hungry birds with idle beaks. A long fir pole is the principal thing needed; have this firmly planted in the ground, with a round platform nailed to it about half way up; the top of an apple barrel with a hole made in the middle and the pole passed through it, secured in place by a few wooden supports, will answer the purpose; further up the pole fasten a cross bar, from which to hang cocoa-nuts, and at the top some twigs should be woven to form a cage to hold the lumps of suet that birds love; threaded strings of monkey-nuts should be hung from the cross bars, and breadcrumbs, seed, and a pan of water should rest on the platform.

15 January

The Garden Seat

Thomas Hardy (1840–1928)

Its former green is blue and thin,
And its once firm legs sink in and in;
Soon it will break down unaware,
Soon it will break down unaware.

At night when reddest flowers are black
Those who once sat thereon come back;
Quite a row of them sitting there,
Quite a row of them sitting there.

With them the seat does not break down,
Nor winter freeze them, nor floods drown,
For they are as light as upper air,
They are as light as upper air!

Tradition

From *Dr Thorne, 1858* | Anthony Trollope (1815–1882)

Greshamsbury House stands amid a multitude of trim gardens
and stone-built terraces, divided one from another: these to our
eyes are not so attractive as that broad expanse of lawn by which
our country houses are generally surrounded; but the gardens
of Greshamsbury have been celebrated for two centuries, and
any Gresham who would have altered them would have been
considered to have destroyed one of the well-known landmarks
of the family.

17 January

A Second Chance

From *In the Eye of the Garden, 1993* | Mirabel Osler (1925–2016)

Gardening is unique in many ways. Not only for the personal
aura which it manifests, but because it is an occupation to which
there is no end. Gardeners are always on their way, but never
arriving. Unlike the poet or the architect, we cannot walk away
from our creations. What a writer writes remains on the page, the
painter's brushwork, the architect's building, or the composer's
score, passes from one century to another. A garden is temporal.

Yet this is the magic of gardening; we become enthralled
however unaware we are of what is stealthily happening while
we are dividing irises. Gardening is unique, too, for giving us
a second chance. That doesn't often happen in life. You cannot
have another go with a job you have bungled, with the crucial
advice you failed to take, or with the high-rise flats you have
built; or even with a child you despair of, a husband, or the
bailiffs. But gardens, however disastrous, are beneficent. The
return of the seasons allows us to try again. Again and again –
there is no end. What failed last summer can be attempted in the
next. Even as the flower dies it is preparing for revival in spring.
The continual cycle of decay and regeneration gives us forever
the opportunity to broadcast fresh seeds, for there is one intrinsic
truth: a garden never repeats itself. Never again can you have this
year what you achieved in the last.

To be done in the Parterre and Flower Garden: Traps, Rain, Snow and Frost

From *Kalendarium Hortense, 1664* | John Evelyn (1620–1706)

Set up your *Traps for Vermine*; especially in your *Nurseries* of *Kernels* and *Stones*, and amongst your *bulbous Roots*; which will now be in danger. A *Paste* made of coarse *Honey*, wherein is mingled *Green-glass* beaten, with *Copperas*, may be laid near their Haunts. About the middle of this *Month*, plant now your *Anemony Roots*, and *Ranunculus's*, which you will be secure of, without *covering*, or farther trouble: Preserve from too great and continuing *Rains* (if they happen), *Snow*, and *Frost*, your choicest *Anemonies* and *Ranunculus's* sow'd in *September* or *October* for earlier *Flowers*: Also your *Carnations*, and such *Seeds* as are in peril of being wash'd out, or over-*chill'd* and *frozen*, covering them under *shelter*, and striking off the *Snow* where it lies too weighty; for it certainly rots and bursts your early-set *Anemonies* and *Ranunculus's*, *&c.* unless planted now in the *Hot-beds*; for now is the *Season*, and they will *flower* even in *London*. Towards the *end*, earth-up with fresh and light Mould the roots of those *Auricula's* which the *Frosts* may have uncover'd; filling up the *Chinks* about the sides of the *Pots* where your choicest are set, but they need not be *hous'd*: it is a hardy Plant.

Nature and Art

From *The Faerie Queene, 1590* | Edmund Spenser (c.1552–1599)

THE SECOND BOOKE, CANT. XII, VERSES 58–59

There the most daintie Paradise on ground,
  It selfe doth offer to his sober eye,
  In which all pleasures plenteously abound,
  And none does others happinesse enuye:
  The painted flowres, the trees upshooting hye,
  The dales for shade, the hilles for breathing space,
  The trembling groves, the Christall running by;
  And that, which all faire workes doth most aggrace,
The art, which all that wrought, appeared in no place.

One would have thought, (so cunningly, the rude,
  And scorned parts were mingled with the fine,)
  That nature had for wantonesse ensude
  Art, and that Art at nature did repine;
  So striving each th'other to undermine,
  Each did the others worke more beautifie;
  So diff'ring both in willes, agreed in fine:
  So all agreed through sweete diversitie,
This Gardin to adorne with all varietie.

Hedges in Scotland

From *The Scots Gardener, 1683* | John Reid (1656–1723)

As there is no country can have more need of planting than this, so none is more needful of inclosing; for we well know how vain it is to plant, unless we inclose.

The Wish

Verses 1–3 | Abraham Cowley (1618–1667)

Well then; I now do plainly see,
This busie world and I shall ne'er agree;
The very *Honey* of all earthly joy
   Does of all meats the soonest *cloy;*
   And they (methinks) deserve my pity
Who for it can endure the stings,
The *Crowd,* and *Buz,* and *Murmurings*
   Of this great *Hive,* the *City.*

Ah, yet, e're I descend to th'grave
May I a *small House,* and *large Garden* have!
And a *few Friends,* and *many Books,* both true,
   Both wise, and both delightful too
   And since Love ne'r will from me flee,
A *Mistress* moderately fair,
And good as *Guardian-Angels* are,
   Only belov'd, and loving me!

O, *Fountains,* when in you shall I
Myself, eas'd of unpeaceful thoughts, espy?
O *Fields!* O *Woods!* when, when shall I be made
   The happy *Tenant* of your shade?
   Here's the Spring-head of *Pleasures* flood,
Here's wealthy Natures Treasury,
Where all the *Riches* lie, that she
   Has coyn'd and stampt for good.

The Fine Art of Landscape Gardening

From *Treatise on the Theory and Practice of Landscape Gardening: Preface, 1841* | Andrew Jackson Downing (1815–1852)

Although music, poetry, and painting, sister fine arts, have in all enlightened countries sooner arrived at perfection than Landscape Gardening, yet the latter offers to the cultivated mind in its more perfect examples, in a considerable degree a union of all these sources of enjoyment; a species of *harmony*, in a pleasing combination of the most fascinating materials of beauty in natural scenery: *poetic* expression in the babbling brook, the picturesque wood, or the peaceful sun-lit turf: and the lovely effects of landscape *painting*, realized in the rich, varied, and skilfully arranged whole.

The object of this charming art, is to create in the grounds of a country residence a kind of polished scenery, producing a delightful effect, either by a species of studied and elegant *design*, in symmetrical or regular plantations: or by a combination of beautiful or picturesque forms, such as we behold in the most captivating passages of general nature.

The Right Weather

From *The Fables of Aesop, retold by Rev. Thomas James, 1848*

| Aesop (620–564 BC) | Rev. Thomas James (1809–1863)

A FATHER AND HIS TWO DAUGHTERS:

A man had two daughters, married one to a Gardener, the other to a Potter. After a while he paid a visit to the Gardener's, and asked his daughter how she was, and how it fared with her. 'Exceedingly well,' said she; 'we have everything that we want; I have but one prayer, that we may have a heavy storm of rain to water our plants.' Off he set to the Potter's and asked his other daughter how matters went with her. 'There is not a thing we want,' she replied; 'and I only hope this fine weather and hot sun may continue to bake our tiles.' 'Alack,' said the Father, 'if you wish for fine weather, and your sister for rain, which am I to pray for myself?'

A Posy on the Kitchen Table

From *Natural Selection, 2017* | Dan Pearson (1964–)

GERALDINE:

Though Geraldine's plants were not conventionally grown – she had her own pruning style and never bothered if a plant got moth-eaten along the way – she understood how to get the best out of them.

Every day of the year there would be a posy to greet you on the kitchen table. Pushed at random into a little pot or suitable utensil, the posy would be there come rain or shine, and in it there was the reward of adventure, the fruit of labour or the chance happening of something one of her many birds had brought to the garden. In this posy were mapped the weeks of the year. A sprig of *Hamamelis* and *Galanthus* in January, or a tuft of old man's beard and rosehips come autumn. Her posies were the garden distilled in a jam jar, and often she would pluck a sprig that you might admire from the assemblage and push it into your hand as the making of a cutting. She shared her garden well, and to this day I try to keep a posy from my own garden.

The Vegetable or Kitchen Garden: Plans

From *The Beeton Book of Garden Management, 1862* | Samuel
Orchart Beeton (1831–1877)

The work to be done in the kitchen garden in January depends
altogether on the weather. In open frosty weather no opportunity
should be lost for wheeling manure on the vacant ground. All the
refuse about the grounds should be collected and added to the
manure heap, and that burned or charred which will not readily
decompose, and added to it.

This is also the season when the forethought of the gardener may
be exhibited. He has to lay down his plan of operations for the
year, or at least for the next three months; and on his judgment
in doing this much of the successful cultivation depends. If he
cover too much ground with early crops in these three months,
not only will great waste arise, but he will have forestalled the
space required for the main crops in April, May, and June, when
some of the most important crops are to be sown. He should make
his calculations now, so as to secure a constant succession of the
various products as they are required, but leaving little or nothing
to run to waste.

It is a good practice, in going through the orchard, bush fruit, and
trees generally, to cut off all spare wood at this season, assort them
as to size and shape, and tie them up in bundles ready for use as
pea sticks and other purposes.

Lowood

From *Jane Eyre, 1847* | Charlotte Brontë (1816–1855)

The garden was a wide enclosure, surrounded with walls so high
as to exclude every glimpse of prospect; a covered verandah ran
down one side, and broad walks bordered a middle space divided
into scores of little beds: these beds were assigned as gardens
for the pupils to cultivate, and each bed had an owner. When
full of flowers they would doubtless look pretty; but now, at the
latter end of January, all was wintry blight and brown decay. I
shuddered as I stood and looked round me: it was an inclement
day for out-door exercise; not positively rainy, but darkened by a
drizzling yellow fog; all under foot was still soaking wet with the
floods of yesterday.

Naturalistic Style

From *Natural Planting, 1997* | Penelope Hobhouse (1929–)

Basically obvious, but not always considered, is the fact that
plants requiring different sorts of planting situations also often
have distinctly different appearances. They do not look natural
grown together, however much horticultural effort has made
it possible. Silver-leaved artemisia from stony Mediterranean
soil simply looks ridiculous beside moisture-loving large-leaved
rodgersias or gunneras. The nineteenth-century scientist and
explorer Alexander von Humboldt attached special importance
to the appearance of plants – the physiognomy – which relates
to their own particular landscapes, and this can be translated
into gardening.

No-man's Wood

W. H. Davies (1871–1940)

Shall I have jealous thoughts to nurse,
When I behold a rich man's house?
Not though his windows, thick as stars,
  Number the days in every year;
I, with one window for each month,
  Am rich in four or five to spare.

But when I count his shrubberies,
His fountains there, and clumps of trees,
Over the palings of his park
  I leap with my primeval blood;
Down wild ravines to Ocean's rocks,
  Clean through the heart of No-man's Wood.

Temples

From *An Encyclopaedia of Gardening, 1822* | John Claudius Loudon
(1783–1843)

Temples, either models or imitations of the religious buildings
of the Greeks and heathen Romans, are sometimes introduced
in garden scenery to give dignity and beauty. In residences of a
certain aspect and character, they may be admissible as imitations,
as resting places, and as repositories of sculptures or antiquities.
Though their introduction has been brought into contempt by its
frequency, and by bad imitations in perishable materials, yet they
are not for that reason to be rejected by good taste. They may
often add dignity and a classic air to a scene; and when erected
of durable materials, and copied from good models, will, like the
originals, please as independent objects.

No Spot too Small

From *Letters from a Citizen of the World to his Friends in the East, 1760–1761* | Oliver Goldsmith (1728–1774)

EXTRACT: LETTER XXX
From Lien Chi Altangi, to the care of Fipsihi, resident in Moscow, to be forwarded by the Russian caravan to Fum Hoam, first president of the ceremonial academy at Pekin in China.

A very small extent of ground is enough for an elegant taste; the greater room is required if magnificence is in view. There is no spot, though ever so little, which a skilful designer might not thus improve, so as to convey a delicate allegory, and impress the mind with truths the most useful and necessary.

FEBRUARY

Sharp Frosts and Drying Winds

Treasures of Winter

From *The Garden, written 1939–1945, published 1946* | Vita
Sackville-West (1892–1962)

Still may you with your frozen finger cut
Treasures of Winter, if you planted well;
The Winter-sweet against a sheltering wall,
Waxen, Chinese, and drooping bell;
Strange in its colour, almond in its smell;
And the Witch-hazel, *Hamamelis mollis,*
That comes before its leaf on naked bough,
Torn ribbons frayed, of yellow and maroon,
And sharp of scent in frosty English air.

Daffodil and Narcissus

From *Paradisi in Sole Paradisus Terrestris, 1629* | John Parkinson
(1567–1650)

Many idle and ignorant Gardiners and others, who get names
by stealth, as they doe many other things, doe call some of these
Daffodils Narcisses, when as all know that know any Latine,
that Narcissus is the Latine name, and Daffodill the English of
one and the same thing; and therefore alone without any other
Epithite cannot properly distinguish severall things. I would
willingly therefore that all would grow judicious, and call every
thing by his proper English name in speaking English, or else
by such Latine name as every thing hath that hath not a proper
English name, that thereby they may distinguish the severall
varieties of things and not confound them.

John Parkinson

From *Mary's Meadow* in *Aunt Judy's Magazine, 1883–1884*

Juliana Horatia Ewing (1841–1885)

If any readers of 'Mary's Meadow' have been as completely puzzled as the writer was by the title of John Parkinson's old book, it may interest them to know that the question has been raised and answered in *Notes and Queries.*

I first saw the *Paradisi in sole Paradisus* at Kew, some years ago, and was much bewitched by its quaint charm. I grieve to say that I do not possess it; but an old friend and florist – the Rev. H. T. Ellacombe – was good enough to lend me his copy for reference, and to him I wrote for the meaning of the title. But his scholarship, and that of other learned friends, was quite at fault. My old friend's youthful energies (he will permit me to say that he is ninety-four) were not satisfied to rust in ignorance, and he wrote to *Notes and Queries* on the subject, and has been twice answered. It is an absurd play upon words, after the fashion of John Parkinson's day. Paradise, as Aunt Judy's readers may know, is originally an eastern word, meaning a park, or pleasure ground. I am ashamed to say that the knowledge of this fact did not help me with the pun. *Paradisi in sole Paradisus terrestris* means Park – in – son's Earthly Paradise!

Black Frost

From *The Gardener's Year, 1929* | Karel Čapek (1890–1938) |

Translated by Marie Weatherall (1897–1972) and Robert Weatherall (1899–1973)

The gardener is at his worst when the black frosts set in. Then
the earth stiffens and dries to the bone, day after day, and night
after night, deeper and deeper; the gardener thinks of roots which
freeze in the soil, dead and hard as stone; of twigs chilled to the
pith by the dry and icy wind; of the freezing bulbs, into which
in autumn the plant packed all that it had. If I knew that it would
help, I would wrap my holly in my own coat, and draw my pants
over the juniper; I would take off my own shirt for you, Azalea
pontica; I would cover you with my hat, Alum Root, and for you,
Coreopsis, nothing is left but my socks: be thankful for them.

To be done in the Parterre and Flower Garden: Carnations and Aviaries

From *Kalendarium Hortense, 1664* | John Evelyn (1620–1706)

Continue *Baits, Vermine-Traps,* &c. Sow *Alaternus* Seeds in *Cases,* or *open Beds;* cover them with *Thorns,* that the *Poultry* scratch them not out. Sow also *Lark-Spurs,* &c.

Now and then *air* your hous'd *Carnations,* in *warm* days especially, and mild *Showers*; but if like to prove *cold,* set them in again at Night.

Furnish (now towards the end) your *Aviaries* with *Birds* before they couple, &c. and hang up Materials for them to build their *Nests* with.

Rosemary

From *Modern Nature, 1991* | Derek Jarman (1942–1994)

MONDAY 6 FEBRUARY, 1989

Rosemary – *Ros marinus,* sea dew – has proved quite hardy here.
My next door neighbour has an ancient gnarled specimen – all
the garden books are emphatic it hates wind, but a more windy
and exposed spot you could not find. Thomas More, who loved
it, wrote, 'As for Rosemarie, I let it run all over my garden
walls, not because bees love it but because it is the herb sacred
to remembrance and therefore to friendship, whence a sprig of it
hath a dumb language.'

The herb was part of Ophelia's bouquet: 'here's rosemary for
remembrance.' Gilded and tied with ribbons it was carried at
weddings; also a sprig was placed in the hands of the dead.

Legend has it that originally its flowers were white until the
day the Virgin Mary laid out her robe to dry on some bushes,
colouring them a heavenly blue.

Tasteful Plans

From *Headlong Hall, 1816* | Thomas Love Peacock (1785–1866)

Mr Milestone had produced his portfolio for the edification
and amusement of Miss Tenorina, Miss Graziosa, and Squire
Headlong, to whom he was pointing out the various beauties of
his plan for Lord Littlebrain's park.

Mr Milestone. This, you perceive, is the natural state of one part
of the grounds. Here is a wood, never yet touched by the finger
of taste; thick, intricate, and gloomy. Here is a little stream,
dashing from stone to stone, and overshadowed with these
untrimmed boughs.

Miss Tenorina. The sweet romantic spot! How beautifully the
birds must sing there on a summer evening!

Miss Graziosa. Dear sister! how can you endure the horrid thicket?

Mr Milestone. You are right, Miss Graziosa: your taste is correct
– perfectly *en règle*. Now, here is the same place corrected –
trimmed – polished – decorated – adorned. Here sweeps a
plantation, in that beautiful regular curve: there winds a gravel
walk: here are parts of the old wood, left in these majestic circular
clumps, disposed at equal distances with wonderful symmetry:
there are some single shrubs scattered in elegant profusion: here
a Portugal laurel, there a juniper; here a laurustinus, there a
spruce fir; here a larch, there a lilac; here a rhododendron, there
an arbutus. The stream, you see, is become a canal: the banks are
perfectly smooth and green, sloping to the water's edge: and there
is Lord Littlebrain, rowing in an elegant boat.

An Inferior Degree of Beauty

From *Mansfield Park, 1814* | Jane Austen (1775–1817)

EDMUND BERTRAM'S VIEW OF IMPROVERS:

Had I a place to new fashion, I should not put myself into the hands of an improver. I would rather have an inferior degree of beauty, of my own choice, and acquired progressively. I would rather abide by my own blunders than by his.

Out in the Garden

Katherine Mansfield (1888–1923)

Out in the garden,
Out in the windy, swinging dark,
Under the trees and over the flower-beds,
Over the grass and under the hedge border,
Someone is sweeping, sweeping,
Some old gardener.
Out in the windy, swinging dark,
Someone is secretly putting in order,
Someone is creeping, creeping.

Yew Cones

From *The Ivington Diaries, 2009* | Monty Don (1955–)

AWAKE AT 2.30AM:

I was entranced by the shapes that the topiary yew cones and
their shadows made in the bright, frosty moonlight. A breeze
rippled the dark like a river and the silvery monochrome stripped
away everything but the shape from the yews. Twenty-six cones,
each different but for that moment each perfect and each with
its shadow like an echo. This was an image that I had never
imagined when I planted them nine years ago. But how many
absolutely clear, frosty days are there in a year when there is also a
full moon? One? Two? And how often are you likely to be up at
2.30 in the morning to enjoy them? It felt like a door had opened
and shown me a parallel garden in another dimension.

10 February

The Problem with Gardeners

From *The Belton Estate, 1865* | Anthony Trollope (1815–1882)

Mrs Winterfield was always unhappy about her gardener. Serious
footmen are very plentiful, and even coachmen are to be found
who, at a certain rate of extra payment, will be punctual at prayer
time, and will promise to read good little books; but gardeners,
as a class, are a profane people, who think themselves entitled
to claim liberty of conscience, and who will not submit to the
domestic despotism of a serious Sunday. They live in cottages
by themselves, and choose to have an opinion of their own on
church matters.

The Glory of the Garden

1911 | Rudyard Kipling (1865–1936)

Our England is a garden that is full of stately views,
Of borders, beds and shrubberies and lawns and avenues,
With statues on the terraces and peacocks strutting by;
But the Glory of the Garden lies in more than meets the eye.

For where the old thick laurels grow, along the thin red wall,
You find the tool- and potting-sheds which are the heart of all;
The cold-frames and the hot-houses, the dungpits and the tanks,
The rollers, carts and drain-pipes, with the barrows and the planks.

And there you'll see the gardeners, the men and 'prentice boys
Told off to do as they are bid and do it without noise;
For, except when seeds are planted and we shout to scare the birds,
The Glory of the Garden it abideth not in words.

And some can pot begonias and some can bud a rose,
And some are hardly fit to trust with anything that grows;
But they can roll and trim the lawns and sift the sand and loam,
For the Glory of the Garden occupieth all who come.

Our England is a garden, and such gardens are not made
By singing: – 'Oh, how beautiful!' and sitting in the shade,
While better men than we go out and start their working lives
At grubbing weeds from gravel-paths with broken dinner-knives.

There's not a pair of legs so thin, there's not a head so thick,
There's not a hand so weak and white, nor yet a heart so sick,
But it can find some needful job that's crying to be done,
For the Glory of the Garden glorifieth everyone.

Then seek your job with thankfulness and work till further orders,
If it's only netting strawberries or killing slugs in borders;
And when your back stops aching and your hands begin to harden,
You will find yourself a partner in the Glory of the Garden.

Oh, Adam was a gardener, and God who made him sees
That half a proper gardener's work is done upon his knees,
So when your work is finished, you can wash your hands and pray
For the Glory of the Garden, that it may not pass away!
And the Glory of the Garden it shall never pass away!

Inside the Garden

From *The Secret Garden, 1911* | Frances Hodgson Burnett (1849–1924)

It was the sweetest, most mysterious-looking place anyone could imagine. The high walls which shut it in were covered with the leafless stems of climbing roses, which were so thick that they were matted together. Mary Lennox knew they were roses because she had seen a great many roses in India. All the ground was covered with grass of a wintry brown and out of it grew clumps of bushes which were surely rose bushes if they were alive. There were numbers of standard roses which had so spread their branches that they were like little trees. There were other trees in the garden, and one of the things which made the place look strangest and loveliest was that climbing roses had run all over them and swung down long tendrils which made light swaying curtains, and here and there they had caught at each other or at a far-reaching branch and had crept from one tree to another and made lovely bridges of themselves. There were neither leaves nor roses on them now and Mary did not know whether they were dead or alive, but their thin grey or brown branches and sprays looked like a sort of hazy mantle spreading over everything, walls, and trees, and even brown grass, where they had fallen from their fastenings and run along the ground. It was this hazy tangle from tree to tree which made it all look so mysterious. Mary had thought it must be different from other gardens which had not been left all by themselves so long; and indeed it was different from any other place she had ever seen in her life.

The Only Flowers

From *The Curious Gardener, 2010* | Anna Pavord (1940–)

TULIPS:

As far as I am concerned, these are the best, indeed the only flowers to send or receive on Valentine's Day. Wild, irrepressible, wayward, unpredictable, strange, subtle, generous, elegant, tulips are everything you would wish for in a lover. Best of all are the crazy parrot tulips such as 'Rococo' with red and pink petals feathered and flamed in crinkly lime-green. 'When a young man presents tulips to his mistress,' wrote Sir John Chardin (*Travels in Persia,* 1686), 'he gives her to understand by the general red colour of the flower, that he is on fire with her beauty, and by the black base, that his heart is burned to coal.' That's the way to do it.

The Promise of Summer

From *Wood and Garden, 1899* | Gertrude Jekyll (1843–1932)

There is always in February some one day, at least, when one smells the yet distant, but surely coming, summer. Perhaps it is a warm, mossy scent that greets one when passing along the southern side of a hedge-bank; or it may be in some woodland opening, where the sun has coaxed out the pungent smell of the trailing ground Ivy, whose blue flowers will soon appear; but the day always comes, and with it the glad certainty that summer is nearing, and that the good things promised will never fail.

15 February

The Vegetable or Kitchen Garden: Preparation

From *The Beeton Book of Garden Management, 1862* | Samuel Orchart Beeton (1831–1877)

The operations on the kitchen garden in February will depend very much on the weather, and must be regulated by it. It is useless to attempt to dig, plant, and sow in wet weather, for the ground will cling in masses to the feet of the workmen, and the time spent in vain attempt will be altogether lost. The hand of the gardener must be withheld until drier weather prevails and the surface of the soil is fairly dry. Then no time must be lost in preparing the ground for, and getting in, the crops for the coming season. Continue to wheel manure onto vacant ground, and get all digging, trenching, and in fact all ground work, as forward as possible, bearing in mind that much of the success of the season depends upon it; and how important it is to have the ground prepared a week or two before cropping, especially where it is heavy or retentive, for none but a practiced workman can appreciate the advantage of having the surface in the finely-pulverised condition that follows sharp frost and drying winds.

To produce carrots and parsnips of an extraordinary size, make a very deep hole with a long dibble; ram the earth well round it while the dibble is in, and when it is removed, fill up the hole with fine rich earth. Sow a few seeds on the top, either parsnips or carrots, as may be required, and when up, draw out all except the one plant nearest to the centre of the hole. Prodigious carrots and parsnips may be produced by this means.

The Moment for Snowdrops

From *Natural Selection, 2017* | Dan Pearson (1964–)

Certain plants are there for a reason: bluebells to light up
woodland with just-sprung green; night-scented stock for those
few heady nights in summer, and apples and sunflowers to remind
us that it has been a good year, a full one with rewards in their
plenty. The snowdrops indicate that the earth is turning, turning
towards a new growing season, even though it feels like there are
weeks to go yet. Pushing decisively from the leaf mould, they
will light up any dark woodland where they have colonised and
claim a moment in deepest winter as their own.

17 February

Green Thumbs

From *Green Thoughts, 1981* | Eleanor Perényi (1918–2009)

People who blame their failures on 'not having a green thumb'
(and they are legion) usually haven't done their homework.
There is of course no such thing as a green thumb. Gardening is
a vocation like any other — a calling, if you like, but not a gift
from heaven. One acquires the necessary skills and knowledge to
do it successfully, or one doesn't. The ancients gardened without
guidance from books, by eye and by hand, and while I am a
devotee of gardening books and love to study and quarrel with
them, I don't think they are a substitute for practical experience,
any more than cookbooks are.

What Is a Garden?

Reginald Arkell (1881–1959)

What is a garden?
  Goodness knows!
You've got a garden
  I suppose:

To one it is a piece of ground
For which some gravel must be found.
To some, those seeds that must be sown,
To some a lawn that must be mown.
To some a ton of Cheddar rocks.
To some it means a window box;
To some, who dare not pick a flower –
A man, at eighteen pence an hour.
To some, it is a silly jest.
About the latest garden pest;
To some, a haven where they find
Forgetfulness and peace of mind . . .

What is a garden
  Large or small,
'Tis just a garden
  After all.

From the Point of View of the Plant

From *English Gardens, 1944* | Harry Roberts (1871–1946)

When I was less than seven years old, I was allotted a small strip of border under a sandstone wall, for my very own, to grow what I liked. Someone had given me a little book called *Gardening for Children*, with coloured plates of flowers; of a number of these I begged cuttings or seeds from my mother and from neighbours. Later, I came across some little books on the natural history of butterflies, beetles and wild flowers. I soon became interested in all these things, and used to hunt for them in the lanes and ditches.

. . . .

I grew more and more interested in the habits of these plants and animals, and was inclined to look at garden plants from the point of view of their likings and 'natural' way of life; getting early to the stage at which that celebrated gardener, Canon Ellacombe, eventually arrived; so that if I found a plant had spread from its position in the border to the middle of the gravel path, where it was obviously more at home, I preferred rather to change the path, than to disturb the plant.

The Fickle Climate

From *In a Gloucestershire Garden, 1895* | Rev. Henry N. Ellacombe
(1822–1916)

I am not fond of frost and snow, and the older we get the less we
like it. But I have no doubt whatever that frost and snow have
their uses, and that we should be all the worse without them.
Many writers have taken the British weather as their theme, and
shown how its endless changes and its harshness have done much
to develop the character of Englishmen, of which an extreme
instance may be taken in Kingsley's eulogy of and welcome to
the north-east wind. But I am speaking only of the effects of
frost and snow on English gardens, and I feel sure, though I may
not be able to prove it, that much of the beauty of our English
gardens comes from our English winters; for certainly our fickle
seasons must have been the determining element in the character
of our gardens, as, indeed, the seasons must be everywhere
throughout the world. But however that may be, there can be
no doubt that the interest of our gardens, and that which has
made Great Britain a nation of gardeners, has been our fickle and
comparatively cold climate.

. . . .

To have a garden where nature and the climate do everything,
and man is called upon to do little more than scratch the ground
and gather the flowers and fruit, might be very pleasant from one
point of view, but it would take away all that to me constitutes
the real interest of gardening, in its difficulties, and even its
disappointments.

Purity of Provenance

From *The Jewel Garden, 2004* | Monty Don (1955–)

Hellebores are the most impressive plants of February and March, with none of the coyness or delicacy that so many spring flowers seem to possess. They are stately and confident, and considered terribly grown up and tasteful. But despite these handicaps you cannot fail to be charmed by them, especially *Helleborus orientalis*, holding their astonishing faces to the ground. The only way to really look at them is to lift each flower head between two fingers or to pick and float them in a shallow bowl of water.

Almost all our hellebores are in the spring garden and form the bulk of the planting in these months. We have some particularly dark Ballard strains in the jewel garden but they can look a little lost and isolated in the otherwise dormant borders. This is a classic case for colour coding becoming a rod for one's back. They are a wonderful rich plum colour so fulfil the jewel-like remit, but hellebores look best en masse and these would certainly enrich their slightly less exalted cousins fifty yards away in the spring garden.

We should really root out all the rather muddy pink seedlings that have self-hybridised because on the whole the nearer to white or black a hellebore flower can be the better it is. We have enough stunning 'pure' varieties to remind me of this every year but I have not the heart for the necessary ethnic cleansing. I like their profligacy and promiscuity, and the way that they grow in a clutter and jumble of sepia-edged pink. Anyway, I am more interested in the way a plant makes me feel than the purity of its provenance.

An Arbour and a Feast

From *The Fall of Hyperion, written 1819, published 1856*
Canto I, lines 19–34 | John Keats (1795–1821)

Methought I stood where trees of every clime,
Palm, myrtle, oak, and sycamore, and beech,
With plantain, and spice blossoms, made a screen;
In neighbourhood of fountains (by the noise
Soft showering in my ears), and, (by the touch
Of scent,) not far from roses. Turning round
I saw an arbour with a drooping roof
Of trellis vines, and bells, and larger blooms,
Like floral censers swinging light in air;
Before its wreathed doorway, on a mound
Of moss, was spread a feast of summer fruits,
Which, nearer seen, seem'd refuse of a meal
By angel tasted or our Mother Eve;
For empty shells were scattered on the grass,
And grape stalks but half bare, and remnants more,
Sweet smelling, whose pure kinds I could not know.

Birds and Snowdrops

From *Diary, 1906* | Edith Holden (1871–1920)

FEBRUARY 24:

Cycled to Packwood House through Solihull and Bentley-heath.
I passed a rookery on the way, the Rooks were all very busy
building up their old nests, and a great deal of chatter they made
over it. I saw a little Robin gathering material for its nest, at
one place on the bank, and further on, a Thrush with a beakful
of long straws. Everywhere the branches of the Willow bushes
were tipped with downy white balls and Alder-catkins were
showing very red. In the garden of Packwood Hall, adjoining
the churchyard the borders were full of large clumps of single
snowdrops. I brought away a great bunch.

Bears

From *Waverley, 1814* | Sir Walter Scott (1731–1832)

The southern side of the house, clothed with fruit-trees, and
having many evergreens trained upon its walls, extended its
irregular yet venerable front along a terrace, partly paved, partly
gravelled, partly bordered with flowers and choice shrubs. This
elevation descended by three several flights of steps, placed in
its centre and at the extremities, into what might be called the
garden proper, and was fenced along the top by a stone parapet
with a heavy balustrade, ornamented from space to space with
huge grotesque figures of animals seated upon their haunches,
among which the favourite bear was repeatedly introduced.
Placed in the middle of the terrace between a sashed-door
opening from the house and the central flight of steps, a huge
animal of the same species supported on his head and fore-paws
a sun-dial of large circumference, inscribed with more diagrams
than Edward's mathematics enabled him to decipher.

The garden, which seemed to be kept with great accuracy,
abounded in fruit-trees, and exhibited a profusion of flowers and
evergreens, cut into grotesque forms. It was laid out in terraces,
which descended rank by rank from the western wall to a large
brook, which had a tranquil and smooth appearance, where it
served as a boundary to the garden; but, near the extremity,
leapt in tumult over a strong dam, or wear-head, the cause of
its temporary tranquillity, and there forming a cascade, was
overlooked by an octangular summer-house, with a gilded bear
on the top by way of vane.

Fountains

From *The Essays or Counsels, Civil and Moral: On Gardening, 1625* | Francis Bacon (1561–1626)

For fountains, they are a great beauty and refreshment; but pools mar all, and make the garden unwholesome, and full of flies and frogs. Fountains I intend to be of two natures: the one that sprinkleth or spouteth water; the other a fair receipt of water, of some thirty or forty foot square, but without fish, or slime, or mud. For the first, the ornaments of images gilt, or of marble, which are in use, do well: but the main matter is so to convey the water, as it never stay, either in the bowls or in the cistern; that the water be never by rest discoloured, green or red or the like; or gather any mossiness or putrefaction. Besides that, it is to be cleansed every day by the hand. Also some steps up to it, and some fine pavement about it, doth well. As for the other kind of fountain, which we may call a bathing pool, it may admit much curiosity and beauty; wherewith we will not trouble ourselves: as, that the bottom be finely paved, and with images; the sides likewise; and withal embellished with coloured glass, and such things of lustre; encompassed also with fine rails of low statua's. But the main point is the same which we mentioned in the former kind of fountain; which is, that the water be in perpetual motion, fed by a water higher than the pool, and delivered into it by fair spouts, and then discharged away under ground, by some equality of bores, that it stay little. And for fine devices, of arching water without spilling, and making it rise in several forms (of feathers, drinking glasses, canopies, and the like), they be pretty things to look on, but nothing to health and sweetness.

Waterworks

From *Diary of John Evelyn, 27th February 1644* | John Evelyn
(1620–1706)

By the way, we alighted at St. Cloud, where, on an eminence
near the river, the Archbishop of Paris has a garden, for the
house is not very considerable, rarely watered and furnished
with fountains, statues, and groves; the walks are very fair; the
fountain of Laocoon is in a large square pool, throwing the
water near forty feet high, and having about it a multitude of
statues and basins, and is a surprising object. But nothing is
more esteemed than the cascade falling from the great steps into
the lowest and longest walk from the Mount Parnassus, which
consists of a grotto, or shell-house, on the summit of the hill,
wherein are divers waterworks and contrivances to wet the
spectators; this is covered with a fair cupola, the walls painted
with the Muses, and statues placed thick about it, whereof some
are antique and good. In the upper walks are two perspectives,
seeming to enlarge the alleys, and in this garden are many other
ingenious contrivances.

Everlasting Winter

From *The Selfish Giant*, 1888 | Oscar Wilde (1854–1900)

'Trespassers Will Be Prosecuted'
Then the spring came, and all over the country there were little blossoms and little birds. Only in the garden of the selfish giant it was still winter. The birds did not care to sing in it as there were no children and the trees forgot to blossom. Once a beautiful flower put its head out from the grass, but when it saw the notice-board it was so sorry for the children that it slipped back into the ground again, and went off to sleep. The only people who were pleased were the snow and the frost. 'Spring has forgotten this garden,' they cried, 'so we will live here all the year round.' The snow covered up the grass with her great white cloak, and the frost painted all the trees silver. Then they invited the north wind to stay with them, and he came. He was wrapped in furs, and he roared all day about the garden, and blew the chimney-pots down. 'This is a delightful spot,' he said, 'we must ask the hail on a visit.' So the hail came. Every day for three hours he rattled on the roof of the castle till he broke most of the slates, and then he ran round and round the garden as fast as he could go. He was dressed in grey, and his breath was like ice.

'I cannot understand why the spring is so late in coming,' said the selfish giant, as he sat at the window and looked out at his cold white garden; 'I hope there will be a change in the weather.'

But the spring never came, nor the summer. The autumn gave golden fruit to every garden, but to the giant's garden she gave none. 'He is too selfish,' she said. So it was always winter there, and the north wind, and the hail, and the frost, and the snow danced about through the trees.

Satan's View of the Garden of Eden

From *Paradise Lost, 1667* | John Milton (1608–1674)

Book IV, lines 205–222

Beneath him, with new wonder now he views,
To all delight of human sense exposed,
In narrow room, nature's whole wealth; yea, more –
A heaven on earth: for blissful Paradise
Of God the garden was, by him in the east
Of Eden planted; Eden stretched her line
From Auran eastward to the royal towers
Of great Seleucia, built by Grecian kings,
Or where the sons of Eden long before
Dwelt in Telassar: In this pleasant soil
His far more pleasant garden God ordained;
Out of the fertile ground he caused to grow
All trees of noblest kind for sight, smell, taste;
And all amid them stood the tree of life,
High eminent, blooming ambrosial fruit
Of vegetable gold; and next to life,
Our death, the tree of knowledge, grew fast by,
Knowledge of good bought dear by knowing ill.

MARCH

A Moonlit Path and Beds of Bloom

Catalogue Writers

From *Onward and Upward in the Garden, 1979* | Katharine S. White (1892–1977)

THE NEW YORKER, MARCH 1

For gardeners, this is the season of lists and callow hopefulness; hundreds of thousands of bewitched readers are poring over their catalogues, making lists for their seed and plant orders, and dreaming their dreams. It is the season, too, when the amateur gardener like myself marvels or grumbles at the achievements of the hybridizers and frets over the idiosyncrasies of the editors who get up the catalogues. They are as individualistic – these editors and writers – as any Faulkner or Hemingway, and they can be just as frustrating or rewarding. They have an audience equal to the most popular novelist's, and a handful of them are stylists of some note. Even the catalogues with which no one man can be associated seem to have personalities of their own.

. . . .

Whatever may be said about the seedsmen's and nurserymen's methods, their catalogue writers are my favorite authors and produce my favorite reading matter. Most of them write anonymously, but a few men who sign their names offer fine examples of regional literature.

The Dividing Line

From *The Book of Old-Fashioned Flowers, 1901* | Harry Roberts
(1871–1946)

The dividing line between the seasons is, of course, quite arbitrary, for Nature progresses evenly, gradually, unceasingly, and not in the jerky way which our clumsy divisions of time imply. Still it is convenient, almost necessary indeed, to adopt some such broad classification of the periods of the year as that into the four seasons which has done duty for so many centuries. One may take the flowering of the snowdrop to indicate the onset of spring, though itself belonging more especially to winter. Yet the Dutch Crocus seems to be the earliest real spring flower, and a brighter little herald of the glories to follow could not be selected.

2 March

The Vexations of a Kitchen Garden

From *Northanger Abbey, written 1803, published 1817* | Jane Austen (1775–1817)

CATHERINE IS SHOWN THE KITCHEN GARDEN AT NORTHANGER ABBEY:

The number of acres contained in this garden was such as Catherine could not listen to without dismay, being more than double the extent of all Mr Allen's, as well as her father's, including church-yard and orchard. The walls seemed countless in number, endless in length; a village of hot-houses seemed to arise among them, and a whole parish to be at work within the enclosure. The general was flattered by her looks of surprise, which told him almost as plainly, as he soon forced her to tell him in words, that she had never seen any gardens at all equal to them before; and he then modestly owned that, 'without any ambition of that sort himself, without any solicitude about it, he did believe them to be unrivalled in the kingdom. If he had a hobby-horse, it was *that*. He loved a garden. Though careless enough in most matters of eating, he loved good fruit — or if he did not, his friends and children did. There were great vexations, however, attending such a garden as his. The utmost care could not always secure the most valuable fruits. The pinery had yielded only one hundred in the last year. Mr Allen, he supposed, must feel these inconveniences as well as himself.'

'No, not at all. Mr Allen did not care about the garden, and never went into it.'

With a triumphant smile of self-satisfaction, the general wished he could do the same, for he never entered his, without being vexed in some way or other, by its falling short of his plan.

Kitchen-Gardens

From *The English Gardener, 1829* | William Cobbett (1763–1835)

If well managed, nothing is more beautiful than the kitchen-garden: the earliest blossoms come there: we shall in vain seek for flowering shrubs in March, and early in April, to equal the peaches, nectarines, apricots and plums; late in April, we shall find nothing to equal the pear and the cherry; and, in May, the dwarf, or espalier, apple-trees, are just so many immense garlands of carnations. The walks are unshaded: they are not greasy or covered with moss, in the spring of the year, like those in shrubberies: to watch the progress of the crops is by no means unentertaining to any rational creature; and the kitchen-garden gives you this all long before the ornamental part of the garden affords you anything worth looking at. Therefore, I see no reason for placing the kitchen-garden in some out-of-the-way place, at a distance from the mansion house, as if it were a mere necessary evil, and unworthy of being viewed by the owner. In the time of fruiting, where shall we find anything much more beautiful to behold than a tree loaded with cherries, peaches, or apricots, but particularly the two latter?

My Garden

T. E. Brown (1830–1897)

A garden is a lovesome thing, God wot!
Rose plot,
Fringed pool,
Ferned grot –
The veriest school
Of peace; and yet the fool
Contends that God is not –
Not God! in gardens! When the eve is cool?
Nay, but I have a sign;
'Tis very sure God walks in mine.

5 March

The Kitchen Garden

From *The Introduction to the 1895 edition of Maria Edgeworth's Castle Rackrent, 1800* | Anne Thackeray Ritchie
(1837–1919)

A VISIT TO EDGEWORTHSTOWN:

The great Irish kitchen garden, belonging to the house, with its seven miles of wall, was also not unlike a part of a fairy tale.

. . . .

After breakfast we went out into the grounds and through an arched doorway into the kitchen garden. It might have been some corner of Italy or the South of France; the square tower of the granary rose high against the blue, the gray walls were hung with messy fruit trees, pigeons were darting and flapping their wings, gardeners were at work, the very vegetables were growing luxuriant and romantic and edged by thick borders of violet pansy.

6 March

Meg's Plans

From *Little Women, 1868–9* | Louisa May Alcott (1832–1888)

It was a tiny house, with a little garden behind, and a lawn about
as big as a pocket-handkerchief in front. Here Meg meant to have
a fountain, shrubbery, and a profusion of lovely flowers; though
just at present the fountain was represented by a weather-beaten
urn, very like a dilapidated slop-bowl; the shrubbery consisted of
several young larches, undecided whether to live or die, and the
profusion of flowers was merely hinted by regiments of sticks, to
show where seeds were planted.

7 March

Different Views

From *The Art of Beautifying Suburban Home Grounds of Small Extent, 1870* | Frank J. Scott (1828–1918)

There is no way in which men deprive themselves of what costs them nothing and profits them much, more than by dividing their improved grounds from their neighbors, and from the view of passers on the road, by fences and hedges. The beauty obtained by throwing front grounds open together, is of that excellent quality which enriches all who take part in the exchange, and makes no man poorer. As a merely business matter it is simply stupid to shut out, voluntarily, a pleasant lookout through a neighbor's ornamental grounds. If, on the other hand, such opportunities are improved, and made the most of, no gentleman would hesitate to make return for the privilege by arranging his own ground so as to give the neighbor equally pleasing vistas into or across it. It is unchristian to hedge from the sight of others the beauties of nature which it has been our good fortune to create or secure; and all the walls, high fences, hedge screens and belts of trees and shrubbery *which are used for that purpose only,* are so many means by which we show how unchristian and unneighborly we can be. It is true these things are not usually done in any mere spirit of selfishness: they are the conventional forms of planting that come down to us from feudal times, or that were necessary in gardens near cities, and in close proximity to populous neighborhoods with rude improvements and ruder people. It is a peculiarity of English gardens, which it is as unfortunate to follow as it would be to imitate the surly self-assertion of English travelling-manners. An English garden is 'a love of a place' to get into, and an Englishman's heart is warm and hospitable at his own fire-side; but these facts do not make it less uncivil to bristle in strangers' company, or to wall and hedge a lovely garden against the longing eyes of the outside world.

Fences in America

From *Second Nature, 1991* | Michael Pollan (1955–)

The American prejudice against fences predates the suburban development. Fences have always seemed to us somehow un–American. Europeans built walled gardens; Americans from the start distrusted the *hortus conclusus*. If the space within the wall was a garden, then what was outside that wall? To the Puritans the whole American landscape was a promised land, a sacred space, and to draw lines around sections of it was to throw this paramount idea into question. When Anne Bradstreet, the Massachusetts colony's first poet, set about writing a traditional English garden ode, she tore down the conventional garden wall – or (it comes to the same thing) made it capacious enough to take in the whole of America. The Puritans had not crossed the Atlantic to redeem some small, walled plot of land; that they could have done in England. They, or rather God acting through them, had plans for all of it.

Defiance to Winter

From *The Tenth Muse, The four Seasons of the Yeare: Spring,*
1650 | Anne Bradstreet (c.1612–1672)

Sweet Spring, like man in his minority,

At present claim'd and had priority,

With smiling Sun-shine face, and garments green,

She gently thus began, like some fair Queen;

Three months there are allotted to my share,

March, April, May, of all the rest most faire;

Tenth o' th' first, Sol into *Aries* enters,

And bids defiance to all tedious Winters

And now makes glad those blinded Northern wights,

Who for some months have seen but starry lights,

Crosses the line, and equals night and day,

Stil adds to th' last, til after pleasant May;

Now goes the Plow-man to his merry toyl,

For to unloose his Winter-locked soyl,

The Seeds-man now, doth lavish out his Grain,

In hope, the more he casts, the more to gain;

The Gardner, now superfluous branches lops,

And Poles erects, for his green clambering Hops.

Now digs, then sows, his herbs, his flowers and roots

And carefully manures his trees of fruits.

The Pleiades, their influence now give,

And all that seem'd as dead, afresh do live.

89

Spring Frost

From *Shirley, 1849* | Charlotte Brontë (1816–1855)

Spring evenings are often cold and raw, and though this had been
a fine day, warm even in the morning and meridian sunshine,
the air chilled at sunset, the ground crisped, and ere dusk a hoar
frost was insidiously stealing over growing grass and unfolding
bud. It whitened the pavement in front of Briarmains (Mr Yorke's
residence), and made silent havoc among the tender plants in
his garden, and on the mossy level of his lawn. As to that great
tree, strong-trunked and broad-armed, which guarded the gable
nearest the road, it seemed to defy a spring-night frost to harm
its still bare boughs; and so did the leafless grove of walnut-trees
rising tall behind the house.

Planting

From *The Well-Tempered Garden, 1970* | Christopher Lloyd
(1921–2006)

When planting, one of the likeliest faults is that the hole made
will be too small for the plant going into it. Some gardeners will
try to get round this by twirling the plant round so that its roots
are forced in with a spiral twist. But if the roots are spread out
naturally, the plant has a much securer purchase on the ground
and is less likely to get rocked by wind and lifted by frost. Others
push the centre of the plant into the hole and fill it quickly, while
a conveniently glazed vision ignores the root-tips that are left
waving about in mid-air. The motto here is to fit the hole to the
plant, not the plant to the hole.

12 March

A Tool Shed

From *Gardening for the Ignorant, 1912* | Mrs Earle (1836–1925) and Ethel Case

Every garden of a certain size, to be comfortable to work in, must have a tool shed with a broad bench for potting and a few shelves and large nails in the walls for hanging up the tools. If there is no room in the shed the roller can be kept outside under a piece of corrugated iron; the mowing machine, well greased, will be best under the bench for the winter. If there are woods of larch trees near you a shed built of split poles will be inexpensive and look very nice, but any wood-merchant would supply the ends of planks or the refuse from coffin-making very cheap, they taper a little at the ends, but are laid one over the other and when the whole is tarred or else painted with jodelite (which has the same quality as tar but is a nice brown colour) the whole looks very well.

13 March

A Contemplation upon Flowers

Henry King (1592–1669)

Brave flowers, that I could gallant it like you
And be as little vaine;
You come abroad, and make a harmless shew,
And to your bedds of Earth againe;
You are not proud, you know your birth
For your Embroiderd garments are from Earth.

You doe obey your months, and times, but I
Would have it ever springe,
My fate would know noe winter, never dye,
Nor thinke of such a thing;
Oh that I could my bed of Earth but view
And Smile, and looke as chearefully as you:

Oh teach me to see death and not to feare
But rather to take truce;
How often have I seene you at a Beere,
And there looke fresh and spruce;
You fragrant flowers then teach me that my breath
Like yours may sweeten, and perfume my death.

Ambitious Aims

From *The Juvenile Gardener, 1824* | Written by a Lady for the use of her own Children, with a view to giving them an early taste for the Pleasures of a Garden and the Study of Botany.

FRANK, AGED 6, IS GIVEN A GARDEN PLOT AND TELLS WILLIAM THE GARDENER WHAT HE WOULD LIKE GROW:

'Master Frank,' said William, 'what do you intend to have in your garden this summer?'

'Oh,' said Frank, 'I must have roses, and tulips, and peas, and cabbages, and fine fruits, and all kinds of things that grow.'

'Then,' said William, 'let me explain to you why you cannot have all you wish this year. As for tulips, it is now too late to plant them, and if we planted rose-trees, they would not bear flowers this summer: then fruit-trees would take up more room than you have to spare; so I fancy you must be content with a few vegetables, and some flowers which will grow from seeds sown this month, and I promise you we shall have variety enough.'

'I am quite content,' said Frank; 'and papa promised, that if I attended your instructions this summer, I should have a larger piece of ground next spring.'

The Vegetable or Kitchen Garden: Planting

From *The Beeton Book of Garden Management, 1862* | Samuel Orchart Beeton (1831–1877)

During this month the great operations of the year are commenced, and most of the principal crops got in. Hitherto, warm and sheltered spots and borders have been appropriated, but the larger quarters have been dug up into ridges, and as large a surface as possible exposed to atmospheric influences. Now the whole garden is to be cropped upon a carefully-considered plan, so that no crop of the same character should follow on the same spot; but having once laid down a well-devised plan for the season, the operations should become comparatively easy. Assuming, therefore, that the previous directions have been attended to, that the soil was turned over in autumn, that it has been frozen, the surface turned over and frozen again, and dried by the winds that generally occur early this month, it is now ready for cropping.

Cardoons: The plant grows very large, after the manner of the globe artichoke. Much room is required for banking-up; accordingly, some gardeners recommend placing them five feet apart at the final planting; but the crop can never pay for this enormous extent of ground.

The Fruit Garden Path

Amy Lowell (1874–1925)

The path runs straight between the flowering rows,
    A moonlit path, hemmed in by beds of bloom,
    Where phlox and marigolds dispute for room
With tall, red dahlias and the briar rose.
'Tis reckless prodigality which throws
    Into the night these wafts of rich perfume
    Which sweep across the garden like a plume.
Over the trees a single bright star glows.
    Dear garden of my childhood, here my years
Have run away like little grains of sand;
    The moments of my life, its hopes and fears
Have all found utterance here, where now I stand;
    My eyes ache with the weight of unshed tears,
You are my home, do you not understand?

Sky-High Beans, Overnight

From *Jack and the Beanstalk, The Red Fairy Book: 1890*

Andrew Lang (1844–1912)

At daybreak Jack rose and went out into the garden. 'At least,' he thought, 'I will sow the wonderful beans. Mother says that they are just common scarlet runners, and nothing else; but I may as well sow them.' So he took a piece of stick, and made some holes in the ground, and put in the beans.

That day they had very little dinner, and went sadly to bed, knowing that for the next day there would be none, and Jack, unable to sleep from grief and vexation, got up at day-dawn and went out into the garden.

What was his amazement to find that the beans had grown up in the night, and climbed up and up until they covered the high cliff that sheltered the cottage and disappeared above it! The stalks had twined and twisted themselves together until they formed quite a ladder.

Mosaic Beds

From *Lothair*, 1870 | Benjamin Disraeli (1804–1881)

'How I hate modern gardens!' said St. Aldegonde. 'What a horrid thing this is! One might as well have a mosaic pavement there. Give me cabbage-roses, sweet-peas, and wall-flowers. That is my idea of a garden. Corisande's garden is the only sensible thing of the sort.'

'One likes a mosaic pavement to look like a garden,' said Euphrosyne, 'but not a garden like a mosaic pavement.'

'The worst of these mosaic beds,' said Madame Phoebus, 'is, you can never get a nosegay, and if it were not for the kitchen-garden, we should be destitute of that gayest and sweetest of creations.'

Winter Is Past

From *The Song of Solomon 2: 11–13* | The King James Bible, 1611

For, lo, the winter is past, the rain is over and gone;

The flowers appear on the earth; the time of the singing of birds is come, and the voice of the turtle is heard in our land;

The fig tree putteth forth her green figs, and the vines with the tender grape give a good smell.

Equinox

From *The Ivington Diaries, 2009* | Monty Don (1955–)

Today is the best day of the year. There is no other calendar
day that is such a cast-iron, sure-fire cert to raise the spirits.
Christmas and birthdays pale into anticlimactic insignificance.
It doesn't matter what the weather is like or what actually
happens, the gift of an extra hour's light at the end of the day is
a prize beyond price. Today stands like a see-saw in the calendar,
balanced exactly on the fulcrum of night and day, and then
tomorrow gently tips towards the light, spilling the days down
into sunshine.

21 March

The Importance of a Good View

From *Pride and Prejudice, 1813* | Jane Austen (1775–1817)

Mr Collins invited them to take a stroll in the garden, which
was large and well laid out, and to the cultivation of which he
attended himself. To work in this garden was one of his most
respectable pleasures; and Elizabeth admired the command of
countenance with which Charlotte talked of the healthfulness of
the exercise, and owned she encouraged it as much as possible.
Here, leading the way through every walk and cross walk, and
scarcely allowing them an interval to utter the praises he asked
for, every view was pointed out with a minuteness which left
beauty entirely behind. He could number the fields in every
direction, and could tell how many trees there were in the most
distant clump. But of all the views which his garden, or which the
country or kingdom could boast, none were to be compared with
the prospect of Rosings, afforded by an opening in the trees that
bordered the park nearly opposite the front of his house. It was a
handsome modern building, well situated on rising ground.

Visiting Gardens

From *Pot-Pourri from a Surrey Garden, 1897* | Mrs Earle
(1836–1925)

Not the least delightful part, in my opinion, of the growing
knowledge of gardening is the appreciative visiting of gardens
of others. On first going into a garden one knows by instinct,
as a hound scents the fox, if it is going to be interesting or not.
One's eyes are sharp, and a joyful glow of satisfaction comes
over one on seeing something not by any means necessarily new,
but unknown to oneself. When looking through old books or
modern catalogues, one feels one has nothing in one's garden,
but I must confess that visiting other people's gardens very often
makes me feel I really have a very fair collection.

23 March

Nebuchadnezzar's Fabled Palace at Babylon

Berossus quoted by Titus Flavius Josephus, 1st century AD

| Berossus, priest of Bel Marduk, active at the beginning of the 3rd century BC |

Titus Flavius Josephus (c.37–100 AD)

When he had thus admirably fortified the city, and had magnificently adorned the gates, he added also a new palace to those in which his forefathers had dwelt, adjoining them, but exceeding them in height and splendor. Any attempt to describe it would be tedious: yet notwithstanding its prodigious size and magnificence it was finished within fifteen days. In this palace he erected very high walks, supported by stone pillars; and by planting what was called a pensile paradise, and replenishing it with all sorts of trees, he rendered the prospect an exact resemblance of a mountainous country. This he did to gratify his queen, because she had been brought up in Media, and was fond of a mountainous situation.

Changes

From *Garden Notebook, 1988* | Beth Chatto (1923–2018)

It is always refreshing to go out and make changes in the garden. I am revitalised as I make plans for next week, next year, or many years ahead. For too long, certain parts of the garden have lain in abeyance, waiting to be redesigned. Sometimes changes are needed to make the garden more labour-saving. Or an area may be grassed over to create a more restful effect. But most enjoyable are the spaces I clear to make homes for more plants and to create new groupings, possibly with introductions I have not grown before.

25 March

New Feet Within My Garden Go

Emily Dickinson (1830–1886)

New feet within my garden go –
New fingers stir the sod –
A Troubadour upon the Elm
Betrays the solitude.

New children play upon the green –
New Weary sleep below –
And still the pensive Spring returns –
And still the punctual snow!

Pliny's Villa at Laurentum

From *Letter to Gallus, Letters Book Two, published during Pliny's lifetime* | Pliny the Younger (61/62–c.113 AD) | Translated by John B. Firth (1868–1943)

The exercise ground has a border of boxwood, or rosemary where the box does not grow well – for box thrives admirably when it is sheltered by buildings, but where it is fully exposed to wind and weather and to the spray of the sea, though it stands at a great distance therefrom, it is apt to shrivel. On the inside ring of the exercise ground is a pretty and shady alley of vines, which is soft and yielding even to the bare foot. The garden itself is clad with a number of mulberry and fig-trees, the soil being specially suitable for the former trees, though it is not so kindly to the others.

To be done in the Parterre and Flower Garden: A Critical Time

From *Kalendarium Hortense, 1664* | John Evelyn (1620–1706)

Stake and *bind* up your weakest *Plants* and *Flowers* against the Winds, before they come too fiercely, and in a moment *prostrate* a whole *Years* Labour.

. . . .

Now you may set your *Oranges*, *Lemmons*, Myrtles . . . and like tender Trees and Plants in the *Portico*, or with the *Windows* and *Doors* of the *Greenhouses* and *Conservatories* open, for eight to ten days before *April*, or earlier, if the *Season* invite (that is, if the sharp *Winds* be past) to acquaint them gradually with the *Air*; I say, gradually and carefully; for this change is the most *Critical* of the whole Year; trust not therefore the *Nights* too confidently, unless the *Weather* be thorowly settled.

The Division of Labour

From *Lark Rise, 1939* | Flora Thompson (1876–1947)

The women never worked in the vegetable gardens or on the allotments, even when they had their children off hand and had plenty of spare time, for there was a strict division of labour and that was 'men's work'. Victorian ideas, too, had penetrated to some extent, and any work outside the home was considered unwomanly. But even that code permitted a woman to cultivate a flower garden, and most of the houses had at least a narrow border beside the pathway. As no money could be spared for seeds or plants, they had to depend upon roots and cuttings given by their neighbours, and there was little variety; but they grew all the sweet old-fashioned cottage garden flowers, pinks and sweet williams and love-in-a-mist, wallflowers and forget-me-nots in spring and hollyhocks and Michaelmas daisies in autumn. Then there were lavender and sweetbriar bushes, and southernwood, sometimes called 'lad's love', but known there as 'old man'.

Almost every garden had its rose bush; but there were no coloured roses amongst them. Only Old Sally had those; the other people had to be content with that meek, old-fashioned white rose with a pink flush at the heart known as the 'maiden's blush'. Laura used to wonder who had imported the first bush, for evidently slips of it had been handed round from house to house.

Narcissus

From *The English Flower Garden, 1883* | William Robinson
(1838–1935)

Daffodil: Beautiful bulbous flowers of mountain and alpine pastures, plains, or woods, thriving admirably in most parts of our island; if anywhere, better in the cooler northern parts and in Ireland, though excellent in cool soils in the south. They are to the spring what Roses, Irises, and Lilies are to summer, what Sunflowers and Chrysanthemums are to autumn, and what Hellebores and Aconite are to winter. No good garden should be without the best of the lovely varieties now known. Narcissi vary so much in form, size, colour, and in time of flowering, that a most attractive spring garden could be made with them alone; provided one had suitable soil, and a background of fresh turf, shrubs, and trees. The best of the commoner kinds should be planted by the thousand, and, indeed, in many cases this has been done with the best results. On grassy banks, on turfy bosses near the roots of lawn-trees, or in meadows near the house, their effect is delightful.

Blight

Edna St Vincent Millay (1892–1950)

Hard seeds of hate I planted
　　That should by now be grown,–
Rough stalks, and from thick stamens
　　A poisonous pollen blown,
And odors rank, unbreathable,
　　From dark corollas thrown!

At dawn from my damp garden
　　I shook the chilly dew;
The thin boughs locked behind me
　　That sprang to let me through,
The blossoms slept,– I sought a place
　　Where nothing lovely grew.

And there, when day was breaking,
　　I knelt and looked around:
The light was near, the silence
　　Was palpitant with sound;
I drew my hate from out my breast
　　And thrust it in the ground.

Oh, ye so fiercely tended,
    Ye little seeds of hate!
I bent above your growing
    Early and noon and late,
Yet are ye drooped and pitiful,–
    I cannot rear ye straight!

The sun seeks out my garden,
    No nook is left in shade,
No mist nor mold nor mildew
    Endures on any blade,
Sweet rain slants under every bough:
    Ye falter, and ye fade.

APRIL

A Jumble of Spring and Summer

Home Thoughts from Abroad

Robert Browning (1812–1889)

I

Oh, to be in England
Now that April's there,
And whoever wakes in England
Sees, some morning, unaware,
That the lowest boughs and brushwood sheaf
Round the elm-tree bole are in tiny leaf,
While the chaffinch sings on the orchard bough
In England — now!

II

And after April, when May follows,
And the whitethroat builds, and all the swallows!
Hark, where my blossomed pear-tree in the hedge
Leans to the field and scatters on the clover
Blossoms and dewdrops — at the bent spray's edge —
That's the wise thrush; he sings each song twice over,
Lest you should think he never could recapture
The first fine careless rapture!
And though the fields look rough with hoary dew
All will be gay when noontide wakes anew
The buttercups, the little children's dower
 — Far brighter than this gaudy melon-flower!

The Reason Flowers Don't Talk

From *Through the Looking-Glass, 1871* | Lewis Carroll (1832–1898)

This time she came upon a large flower-bed, with a border of daisies, and a willow-tree growing in the middle.

'O Tiger-lily!' said Alice, addressing herself to one that was waving gracefully about in the wind, 'I wish you could talk!'

'We can talk,' said the Tiger-lily: 'when there's anybody worth talking to.'

Alice was so astonished that she could not speak for a minute: it quite seemed to take her breath away. At length, as the Tiger-lily only went on waving about, she spoke again, in a timid voice — almost in a whisper. 'And can all the flowers talk?'

'As well as you can,' said the Tiger-lily. 'And a great deal louder.'

Conversations with Fruit-Trees

From *A Dialogue (or Familiar Discourse) Between the Husbandman and Fruit-Trees in his Nurseries, Orchards, and Gardens, 1676* | Ralph Austen (c.1612–1676)

Husbandman: I have read in Learned and Godly mens works and the Scriptures also declare as much; that *yee Fruit-trees can speake, and discourse with men.*

. . . .

What *Language* is it that yee speake, is it *English,* or *Latin,* or *Hebrew,* or what other *Language* else, wherein yee discourse with men.

Fruit-trees: We can speake all *Languages;* We can discourse with any *People,* or *Nation,* in any Language whatsoever; according as people please to discourse with us, so we Answer them; every man in his owne Language.

. . . .

Fruit-Trees: Many people (of all sorts) come from time, to time, and walk among us, and look upon us, and commend us, for brave handsome Trees, lovely, and beautifull, especially when we are in our Gallantries, full of *beautifull blossoms and pleasant, wholesome Fruits;* and some greedily pluck us, and tear us, and sometimes breake off some of our Branches, to get our Fruits; and so go their waies; But speake never a word to us; neither do they understand what we say to them.

Talking to Plants

John Agard (1949–)

Always talk to your plants.
Sit back and watch them flourish.
Good advice. Of course we presume
that all plants speak English.

Speak slowly, watch them bloom.
If necessary shout each syllable.
Their little ears are ready vessels
for a shower of the Queen's vowels.

Never mind if it's a China rose
or an African violet.
Better yet, recite a bit of English Lit.
See abundance spring at your fingertip.

So I spoke like an Oxford don
to my wilting rhododendron.
It wilted more. As for my drooping shrub,
my words only seem to draw more slugs.

O plants, what is it that makes you grow?
I watch my immigrant neighbour's patio
with a sense of distant envy.
Tell me, plants, must I address you in Punjabi?

To Protect All Seeds

From *The Gardener's Labyrinth, 1577* | Thomas Hill (c.1528–1574)

All Seedes of the Garden or field are defended, as reporteth
Anatolius, from all injuries and Monsters, if the Husbandman or
Gardener before the committing of the Seedes to the Earth,
dothe infuse them for a time in the juice of the rootes of the
wilde Cucumber.

Evening

From *The Enchanted April, 1922* | Elizabeth Von Arnim (1866–1941)

That evening was the evening of the full moon. The garden was
an enchanted place where all the flowers seemed white. The lilies,
the daphnes, the orange-blossom, the white stocks, the white
pinks, the white roses — you could see these as plainly as in the
daytime; but the coloured flowers existed only as fragrance.

6 April

Change

From *The Education of a Gardener, 1962* | Russell Page (1906–1985)

Unlike painting or sculpture or buildings a garden grows. Its appearance changes – plants mature, some in six weeks, some in six hundred years. There are few gardens that can be left alone. A few years of neglect and only the skeleton of a garden can be traced – the modelling of the ground perhaps, walls or steps, a pool, the massing of trees. Japanese artists working with a few stones and sand four hundred years ago achieved strangely lasting compositions. However there, too, but for the hands that have piously raked the white sand into patterns and controlled the spread of moss and lichens, little would remain.

7 April

The Royal Horticultural Society

From *Pot-Pourri from a Surrey Garden, 1897* | Mrs Earle
(1836–1925)

One of my greatest pleasures in London in the early spring is
going to the exhibition of the Royal Horticultural Society,
at the Drill Hall, Westminster. I think all amateurs who are
keen gardeners ought to belong to this society – partly as an
encouragement to it, and also because the subscriber of even one
guinea a year gets a great many advantages. He can go to these
fortnightly exhibitions, as well as to the great show at the Temple
Gardens in May, free, before the public is admitted. He has the
run of the society's library in Victoria Street; he receives free the
yearly publications, which are a series of most interesting lectures
(I will give some account of them at the end of the year); and he
is annually presented with a certain number of plants.

8 April

Altruism

From *Heath Robinson: How to Make a Garden Grow, 1938* |
W. Heath Robinson (1872–1944) | Written by K. R. G. Browne (1895–1940)

As the majority of poets live in one-room flats or rat-infested garrets, their opportunities for seeking floral inspiration are rather limited. The garden-owner, therefore, who wishes to combine altruism with business can simultaneously benefit mankind and collect a few odd ducats by admitting poets, in small selected batches, to his garden on fine Spring afternoons and letting them brood there until their respective Muses have kicked in with the needful. For this facility the most impoverished verse-maker will gladly pay at the rate of, say, one shilling per brood-hour.

9 April

122

Blossom

From *Amaryllis at the Fair, 1887* | Richard Jefferies (1848–1887)

The finches came to the boughs that hung over the ivy-grown thatch, and sang in the sycamore opposite the door, and in the apple-trees, whose bloom hung down almost to the ground.

These apple-trees, which Iden had planted, flung sackfuls of bloom at his feet. They poured themselves out in abandoned, open-armed, spendthrift, wasteful — perfectly prodigal — quantities of rose-tinted petal; prodigal as a river which flows full to the brim, never questioning but what there will be plenty of water to follow.

10 April

Stowe

From *Observations on Modern Gardening, 1770* | Thomas Whately
(1726–1772)

The whole space is divided into a number of scenes, each
distinguished with taste and fancy; and the changes are so
frequent, so sudden, and complete, the transitions so artfully
conducted, that the same ideas are never continued or repeated to
satiety.

. . . .

In the front of the house is a considerable lawn, open to the
water, beyond which are two elegant Doric pavillions, placed
in the boundary of the garden, but not marking it, though they
correspond to each other; for still further back, on the brow
of some rising grounds without the enclosure, stands a noble
Corinthian arch, by which the principal approach is conducted,
and from which all the gardens are seen, reclining back against
their hills; they are rich with plantations, full of objects, and lying
on both sides of the house almost equally, every part is within a
moderate distance, notwithstanding the extent of the whole.

A Tour

From *Memorandum made on a tour to some of the gardens of England, described by Whately in his book on Gardening (1770), April 1786* | Thomas Jefferson (1743–1826)

ON WHATELY:

While his descriptions, in point of style, are models of perfect elegance and classical correctness, they are as remarkable for their exactness. I always walked over the gardens with his book in my hand, examined with attention the particular spots he described, found them so justly characterized by him as to be easily recognized, and saw with wonder, that his fine imagination had never been able to seduce him from the truth.

BUT ON STOWE:

In the approach to Stowe, you are brought a mile through a straight avenue, pointing to the Corinthian arch and to the house, till you get to the arch, then you turn short to the right. The straight approach is very ill. The Corinthian arch has a very useless appearance, inasmuch as it has no pretension to any destination. Instead of being an object from the house, it is an obstacle to a very pleasing distant prospect.

Tools of the Right Size

From *Cuttings from My Garden Notebooks, 1997* | Graham Stuart
Thomas (1909–2003)

The smaller the garden the more it depends upon hand-tools,
and therefore the quality of these tools assumes great importance.
Beware of getting tools too large for your frame of body. I am of
about average size, and have found by experience, through a long
life of gardening, that more and better work can be done more
easily by using tools of small to moderate size. Not for me are
large spades and forks and shovels – I leave them to the navvies
of gardening.

13 April

Boarders

From *The Diary of a Nobody, 1892* | George Grossmith (1847–1912) &
Weedon Grossmith (1854–1919)

April 14. − Spent the whole of the afternoon in the garden,
having this morning picked up at a bookstall for fivepence a
capital little book, in good condition, on *Gardening*. I procured
and sowed some half-hardy annuals in what I fancy will be
a warm, sunny border. I thought of a joke, and called out
Carrie. Carrie came out rather testy, I thought. I said: 'I have
just discovered we have got a lodging-house.' She replied: 'How
do you mean?' I said: 'Look at the *boarders*.' Carrie said: 'Is that
all you wanted me for?' I said: 'Any other time you would have
laughed at my little pleasantry.' Carrie said: 'Certainly − *at any
other time*, but not when I am busy in the house.'

To be done in the Parterre and Flower Garden: Protection

From *Kalendarium Hortense, 1664* | John Evelyn (1620–1706)

Now do the *farewell Frosts* and *Easterly Winds* prejudice your choicest *Tulips*, and spot them; therefore cover such with *Mats*, or *Canvas*, to prevent *Freckles*, and sometimes destruction. The same care have of your most precious *Anemonies*, *Auricula's*, *Chamae-iris*, *Brumal Jacynths*, early *Cyclamen*, & c. Wrap your shorn *Cypress* tops with Straw *Wisps*, if the *Eastern Blasts* prove very tedious, and forget not to cover with dry *Straw*, or *Pease-hame*, your young exposed *Ever-greens*, as yet Seedlings, such as *Fir*, *Pine*, *Phillyrea*, *Bays*, *Cypress*, &c. till they have pass'd *two* or *three* Years in the *Nursery*, and are fit to be *transplanted*; for the sharp *Easterly* and *Northerly* Winds transpierce and dry them up. Let this also caution you upon all such Extremities of the *Weather*, during the whole *Winter*; but be mindful to uncover them in all benign and tolerable Seasons and Intermissions; it being these acute *Winds*, and seldom or never the hardest *Frosts* or *Snows*, which do the mischief.

15 April

A Forsaken Garden

Algernon Charles Swinburne (1837–1909)

In a coign of the cliff between lowland and highland,
  At the sea-down's edge between windward and lee,
Walled round with rocks as an inland island,
  The ghost of a garden fronts the sea.
A girdle of brushwood and thorn encloses
  The steep square slope of the blossomless bed
Where the weeds that grew green from the graves of its roses
  Now lie dead.

The fields fall southward, abrupt and broken,
  To the low last edge of the long lone land.
If a step should sound or a word be spoken,
  Would a ghost not rise at the strange guest's hand?
So long have the grey bare walks lain guestless,
  Through branches and briars if a man make way,
He shall find no life but the sea-wind's, restless
  Night and day.

The dense hard passage is blind and stifled
  That crawls by a track none turn to climb
To the strait waste place that the years have rifled
  Of all but the thorns that are touched not of time.
The thorns he spares when the rose is taken;
  The rocks are left when he wastes the plain.
The wind that wanders, the weeds wind-shaken,
  These remain.

Not a flower to be pressed of the foot that falls not;
    As the heart of a dead man the seed-plots are dry;
From the thicket of thorns whence the nightingale calls not,
    Could she call, there were never a rose to reply.
Over the meadows that blossom and wither
    Rings but the note of a sea-bird's song;
Only the sun and the rain come hither
    All year long.

The sun burns sere and the rain dishevels
    One gaunt bleak blossom of scentless breath.
Only the wind here hovers and revels
    In a round where life seems barren as death.
Here there was laughing of old, there was weeping,
    Haply, of lovers none ever will know,
Whose eyes went seaward a hundred sleeping
    Years ago.

Heart handfast in heart as they stood, 'Look thither,'
    Did he whisper? 'look forth from the flowers to the sea;
For the foam-flowers endure when the rose-blossoms wither,
    And men that love lightly may die — but we?'
And the same wind sang and the same waves whitened,
    And or ever the garden's last petals were shed,
In the lips that had whispered, the eyes that had lightened,
    Love was dead.

Or they loved their life through, and then went whither?
    And were one to the end — but what end who knows?
Love deep as the sea as a rose must wither,
    As the rose-red seaweed that mocks the rose.
Shall the dead take thought for the dead to love them?
    What love was ever as deep as a grave?
They are loveless now as the grass above them
    Or the wave.

All are at one now, roses and lovers,
    Not known of the cliffs and the fields and the sea.
Not a breath of the time that has been hovers
    In the air now soft with a summer to be.
Not a breath shall there sweeten the seasons hereafter
    Of the flowers or the lovers that laugh now or weep,
When as they that are free now of weeping and laughter
    We shall sleep.

Here death may deal not again for ever;
    Here change may come not till all change end.
From the graves they have made they shall rise up never,
    Who have left nought living to ravage and rend.
Earth, stones, and thorns of the wild ground growing,
    While the sun and the rain live, these shall be;
Till a last wind's breath upon all these blowing
    Roll the sea.

Till the slow sea rise and the sheer cliff crumble,
    Till terrace and meadow the deep gulfs drink,
Till the strength of the waves of the high tides humble
    The fields that lessen, the rocks that shrink,
Here now in his triumph where all things falter,
    Stretched out on the spoils that his own hand spread,
As a god self-slain on his own strange altar,
    Death lies dead.

Mr Rochester and Jane Walk in the Garden

From *Jane Eyre, 1847* | Charlotte Brontë (1816–1855)

'Now *here* (he pointed to the leafy enclosure we had entered) all is real, sweet and pure.'

He strayed down a walk edged with box; with apple trees, pear trees, and cherry trees on one side, and a border on the other full of all sorts of old-fashioned flowers, stocks, sweet-williams, primroses, pansies, mingled with southern wood, sweet-briar, and various fragrant herbs. They were fresh now as a succession of April showers and gleams, followed by a lovely spring morning, could make them: the sun was just entering the dappled east, and his light illumined the wreathed and dewy orchard trees and shone down the quiet walks under them.

17 April

Love in the Valley

Verses 12 and 13 | George Meredith (1828–1909)

Kerchiefed head and chin she darts between her tulips,
    Streaming like a willow grey in arrowy rain:
Some bend beaten cheek to gravel, and their angel
    She will be; she lifts them, and on she speeds again.
Black the driving raincloud breasts the iron gateway:
    She is forth to cheer a neighbour lacking mirth.
So when sky and grass met rolling dumb for thunder
    Saw I once a white dove, sole light of earth.

Prim little scholars are the flowers of her garden,
    Trained to stand in rows, and asking if they please.
I might love them well but for loving more the wild ones:
    O my wild ones! they tell me more than these.
You, my wild one, you tell of honied field-rose,
    Violet, blushing eglantine in life; and even as they,
They by the wayside are earnest of your goodness,
    You are of life's, on the banks that line the way.

Wind-Swayed Bloom

From *Anne of Avonlea, 1909* | L. M. Montgomery (1874–1942)

Beyond were the 'back fields' of the farms that ran out to the
upper Carmody road. Just before them, hemmed in by beeches
and firs but open to the south, was a little corner and in it a
garden . . . or what had once been a garden. A tumbledown stone
dyke, overgrown with mosses and grass, surrounded it. Along
the eastern side ran a row of garden cherry-trees, white as a
snowdrift. There were traces of old paths still and a double line of
rose-bushes through the middle; but all the rest of the space was
a sheet of yellow and white narcissi, in their airiest, most lavish,
wind-swayed bloom above the lush green grasses.

19 April

To a Gardener

Robert Louis Stevenson (1850–1894)

Friend, in my mountain-side demesne,
My plain-beholding, rosy, green
And linnet-haunted garden-ground,
Let still the esculents abound.
Let first the onion flourish there,
Rose among roots, the maiden-fair,
Wine-scented and poetic soul
Of the capacious salad-bowl.
Let thyme the mountaineer (to dress
The tinier birds) and wading cress,
The lover of the shallow brook,
From all my plots and borders look.
Nor crisp and ruddy radish, nor
Pease-cods for the child's pinafore
Be lacking; nor of salad clan
The last and least that ever ran
About great nature's garden-beds.
Nor thence be missed the speary heads
Of artichoke; nor thence the bean
That gathered innocent and green
Outsavours the belauded pea.

These tend, I prithee; and for me,
Thy most long-suffering master, bring
In April, when the linnets sing
And the days lengthen more and more,
At sundown to the garden door.
And I, being provided thus,
Shall, with superb asparagus,
A book, a taper, and a cup
Of country wine, divinely sup.

Weeds

From *In a Gloucestershire Garden, 1895* | Rev. Henry N. Ellacombe
(1822–1916)

I am sorry to say that the April record of the garden would be
very incomplete without some mention of the weeds; for it is
in April they first show themselves, and some of them only in
April. In new gardens it is possible, and not very difficult, to keep
the weeds under; but in old gardens it is almost impossible. It is
an old and very true gardening proverb, that one year's seed is
many years' weed; or as Hamlet laments, 'An unweeded garden
grows to seed,' and so 'things rank and gross in nature possess
it merely.' In the history of an old garden there must have often
been a one year's seed; and there must be in it from time to time
many an unweeded corner. But I have almost an affection for
weeds, a decided affection for some of them, and I have not much
sympathy with those who say that a garden is not worth looking
at unless it is as clean as a newly-swept floor; it is a counsel of
perfection, which I have no great wish to reach. A weed is but a
good plant in the wrong place; I say a *good* plant advisedly, having
a full faith that where nature plants it, it fills a right place. Daisies
are not perhaps in their right place in lawns, but I should be
sorry to see my lawn quite free from them, and so I am sure
would the children.

The Garden

From *The Lark, 1922* | E. Nesbit (1858–1924)

The garden was full of flowers – daffodils, tulips, wallflowers, forget-me-nots, pansies, oxslips, primroses – and on the walls of the house cherry-coloured Japanese quince. The buds of iris and peonies were already fat with promise, and the roses were in leaf and tiny bud.

22 April

137

The Vegetable or Kitchen Garden: Herbs and Runners

From *The Beeton Book of Garden Management, 1862* | Samuel Orchart Beeton (1831–1877)

The herb garden in the present day is somewhat neglected, and yet the culture and curing of simples was formerly part of a lady's education. There was not a lady in the kingdom but made her dill-tea and diet-drink from herbs grown under her own eye. Thyme, sage, spearmint, and marjoram are all pretty, and a special quarter should be set apart for them in our gardens. This would probably recover, for our soups and salads, some of the neglected tarragons, French sorrel, purslain, chervil, dill, and clary, which are only found now in the pages of old herbals. Laid out after a simple geometric design, the herb garden might be rather ornamental than otherwise.

Scarlet runners may be planted at any time in April or May. The seed should be dropped about 4 inches apart, and if a line be selected along the two sides of a walk in the kitchen garden, a very pretty shady avenue may be made. Plant stakes 7 or 8 feet high in the row where the beans are; set 2 or 3 stakes to the yard, and bend them over at the top to form arches. In the spaces between the stakes place pea sticks, to which the runners may at first be trained. The stakes should also be tied together by wands arranged longitudinally, one along the top, and one halfway up each side. When this framework becomes covered with scarlet runners, a very pleasant shady walk will be formed. With a little care in manuring and watering, the runners may be kept green and in bearing till killed by the autumn frosts. The runners will blossom and bear much more freely if the old beans are all removed, and they are not allowed to ripen seed. A mixture of the white Dutch runner with the scarlet runner gives to the avenue a very pretty effect.

Spring and Summer

From *The Enchanted April, 1922* | Elizabeth Von Arnim (1866–1941)

And meanwhile the beautiful golden days were dropping gently
from the second week one by one, equal in beauty with those
of the first, and the scent of beanfields in flower on the hillside
behind the village came across to San Salvatore whenever the air
moved. In the garden that second week the poet's eyed narcissus
disappeared out of the long grass at the edge of the zigzag path,
and wild gladiolus, slender and rose-coloured, came in their
stead, white pinks bloomed in the borders, filling the whole place
with their smoky-sweet smell, and a bush nobody had noticed
burst into glory and fragrance, and it was a purple lilac bush. Such
a jumble of spring and summer was not to be believed in, except
by those who dwelt in those gardens. Everything seemed to be
out together – all the things crowded into one month which in
England are spread penuriously over six.

The Story of the Davidia

From *Aristocrats of the Garden, 1917* | Ernest Henry 'Chinese' Wilson
(1876–1930)

CHINA 1900:

By the middle of April everything was ready to start in quest
of the Davidia. On a half page of a notebook Dr Henry had
sketched a tract of country about the size of New York State and
had marked the spot where he had found growing a single tree of
the Davidia, the only example he had discovered in a trip which
extended over six months and the only one he had ever seen. The
place was among high mountains in the sparsely populated region
bordering the provinces of Hupeh and Szechuan and south of the
mighty Yangtsze River. This locality was my destination and this
solitary tree my sole objective.

. . . .

I took a cross-country road and on the afternoon of the 25th
reached the hamlet of Ma-huang-po and the house where Dr
Henry had stayed when he found the Davidia tree on May 17,
1888. Did the people remember Dr Henry? Did they know
the K'ung-tung (local name of Davidia)? To these and similar
questions they pleasantly answered in the affirmative. Would
some one guide me to the tree? Certainly! We sallied forth, I in
the highest of spirits. After walking about two miles we came
to a house rather new in appearance. Near by was the stump of
Henry's Davidia. The tree had been cut down a year before and
the trunk and branches formed the beams and posts of the house!
I did not sleep during the night of April 25, 1900.

. . . .

On May 19th when collecting near the hamlet of Ta-wan, distant
some five days southwest of Ichang, I suddenly happened upon a
Davidia tree in full flower! It was about fifty feet tall, in outline
pyramidal, and with its wealth of blossoms was more beautiful
than words can portray.

The Imperial Tulips of Ottoman Turkey

From *Better Gardening, 1982* | Robin Lane Fox (1946–)

Once a year, the Vizier would invite the Sultan to inspect the Imperial Tulips. 'Beside every fourth flower', wrote a French ambassador, who witnessed it, 'is stood a candle, level with the bloom and along the alleys are hung cages filled with all kinds of birds'. Where tulips had grown up blind, the gaps were filled with cut flowers placed in bottles. Lamps lit the trellises and dangled on green shrubs which had been lifted from the nearby woods. Mirrors reflected the lights; musicians bowed and blew their way through the Turkish songs of the moment; Sultan, harem, eunuchs and courtiers were guests at the Vizier's expense until the tulips dropped their petals at their feet. One way, you may feel, of making free with public spending which not even the patrons of your Council's park bedding schemes have yet been able to imagine.

Tulips and Anemones

From *Paradisi in Sole Paradisus Terrestris, 1629* | John Parkinson (1567–1650)

But above and beyond all others, the Tulipas may be so matched, one colour answering and setting of another, that the place where they stand may resemble a peece of curious needle-worke, or peece of painting; and I have knowne in a Garden, the Master as much commended for this artificiall forme in placing the colours of Tulipas, as for the goodnessle of his flowers, or any other thing. The divers sorts and colours of Anemones or Winde-flowers may be so ordered like-wise, which are very beautifull, to have the severall varieties planted one neare unto another, that their severall colours appearing in one place will be a very great grace in a Garden, or if they be dispersed among the other sorts of flowers, they will make a glorious shew.

Loveliest of Trees

A Shropshire Lad, II | A. E. Housman (1859–1936)

Loveliest of trees, the cherry now
Is hung with bloom along the bough,
And stands about the woodlands ride
Wearing white for Eastertide.

Now, of my threescore years and ten,
Twenty will not come again,
And take from seventy springs a score,
It only leaves me fifty more.

And since to look at things in bloom
Fifty springs are little room,
About the woodlands I will go
To see the cherry hung with snow.

28 April

Blossom Season

From *Natural Selection, 2017* | Dan Pearson (1964–)

Observe a blossom season and you will see one tree handing over its moment of glory to the next, as the varieties follow on from each other. First the cherry plum to the blackthorn; next the balloon-shaped flowers of the pears; then the delicate sprays of *Amelanchier,* which cross over with the flurry of cherries. These are many and varied and range from the delicate and single to the full-blown confections that are doubled and sugary. After several weeks the cherries finally give way to the crabs and the apples, which are dimmed only by leaves breaking on the trees as spring gives way to summer.

That moment, however, before the blossom breaks, is perhaps the most wondrous. On the news in Japan, the hanami season is charted in blossom maps that mark the movement across the country. I urge you to get a blossom tree if you do not have one, for the chance of witnessing this window of spring. Slowed for a moment, you too can take in the miracle.

29 April

Learning

From The Garden that I Love, 1894 | Alfred Austin (1835–1913)

This morning I saw a *Tiarella,* or Foam Flower, making a very
respectable show, though I can see I have made a mistake in
planting it where it stands. It is too much exposed to the midday sun, and has hardly sufficient moisture about its roots. Next
year it shall be better treated. For there is no gardening without
humility, an assiduous willingness to learn, and a cheerful
readiness to confess you were mistaken. Nature is continually
sending even its oldest scholars to the bottom of the class for
some egregious blunder. But, by the due exercise of patience and
diligence, they may work their way to the top again.

But, indeed, were it not for one's mistakes, one's failures, and
one's disappointments, the love one bears one's garden would
soon perish for lack of sustenance.

30 April

. . . .

The Garden that I Love is very perverse, very incalculable in
its ways – falling at times as much below expectation as at other
exceeding it. They who have no patience with accident, with
waywardness, should not attempt to garden.

MAY

Wreaths of Flowery Perfume

Blushing Borders

From *The Seasons: Spring, 1726-1730* | James Thomson (1700–1748)

At length, the finish'd garden to the view
Its vistas opens, and its alleys green.
Snatch'd through the verdant maze, the hurried eye
Distracted wanders; now the bowery walk
Of covert close, where scarce a speck of day
Falls on the lengthen'd gloom, protracted sweeps:
Now meets the bending sky; the river now
Dimpling along, the breezy-ruffled lake,
The forest darkening round, the glittering spire,
The ethereal mountain, and the distant main.
But why so far excursive? when, at hand,
Along these blushing borders, bright with dew,
And in yon mingled wilderness of flowers,
Fair-handed Spring unbosoms every grace;
Throws out the snowdrop and the crocus first;
The daisy, primrose, violet darkly blue.
And polyanthus of unnumber'd dyes;
The yellow wallflower, stain'd with iron brown;
And lavish stock that scents the garden round:
From the soft wing of vernal breezes shed,
Anemonies, auriculas, enrich'd
With shining meal o'er all their velvet leaves;
And full ranunculas, of glowing red.
Then comes the tulip race, where Beauty plays
Her idle freaks: from family diffused
To family, as flies the father-dust.
The varied colours run; and while they break
On the charm'd eye, the exulting florist marks,
With secret pride, the wonders of his hand.

The View from the Window

From *Anne of Green Gables, 1908* | L. M. Montgomery (1874–1942)

A huge cherry-tree grew outside, so close that its boughs tapped against the house, and it was so thick-set with blossoms that hardly a leaf was to be seen. On both sides of the house was a big orchard, one of apple-trees and one of cherry-trees, also showered over with blossoms; and their grass was all sprinkled with dandelions. In the garden below were lilac-trees purple with flowers, and their dizzily sweet fragrance drifted up to the window on the morning wind.

2 May

The Vegetable or Kitchen Garden: Watering

From *The Beeton Book of Garden Management, 1862* | Samuel Orchart Beeton (1831–1877)

It is not accounted a wise proceeding to begin to water vegetables, for if you begin to do so you will have to continue it. Some vegetables, too, will present a very bad appearance under intermittent watering, for example, onions, whose tube-like leaves will turn yellow at the top, if water is given to them and subsequently withheld. Nevertheless, all transplanted vegetables must be watered plentifully, and even shaded if facilities exist for affording them shelter from the sun's rays, in order to prevent too great a check to their growth.

Plans for the Garden

From *The Lark, 1922* | E. Nesbit (1858–1924)

A very happy evening was spent over the gardening book. Lucilla made a list of the seeds that would be wanted to carry out what was really a quite brilliant scheme for a year's flower-growing.

'Perhaps you're right,' she owned; 'something might be done with this garden. And there'll be all the soft fruit coming along in the summer.'

'*Soft fruit?* Yes, that's right, it says so in the book. Currants and raspberries and gooseberries – all the squashy kinds. Hard fruit's the sort on trees – apples and pears. We might make jam, put *"Home Made Jam"* on the board.'

'And *"New Laid Eggs"* if only we had fowls.'

'And *"New Milk"* if we had a cow.'

'And *"Home Cured Bacon"* if we had a pig.'

'And everything that people do sell if only we'd room to grow it – if this were a decent-sized house instead of a chocolate-box.'

A Destructive Frost

From *Garden Book, 1766-1824* | Thomas Jefferson (1743–1826)

1774

MAY 5

a frost which destroyed almost every thing. it killed the wheat, rye, corn, many tobacco plants, and even large saplings. the leaves of the trees were entirely killed. all the shoots of the vine. at Monticello near half the fruit of every kind was killed; and before this no instance had ever occurred of any fruit killed here by the frost. in all other places in the neighborhood the destruction of fruit was total. this frost was general & equally destructive thro the whole country and the neighboring colonies.

A Vernal Lustre

From *The English Garden, 1772–1782* | William Mason (1724–1797)

Book the Third, lines 136–148

Nor are the plants which England calls her own
Few, or unlovely, that, with laurel join'd,
And kindred foliage of perennial green,
Will form a close-knit curtain. Shrubs there are
Of bolder growth, that, at the Spring's first call,
Burst forth in blossom'd fragrance. Lilacs rob'd
In snow-white innocence, or purple pride,
The sweet Syringa yielding but in scent
To the rich Orange, or the woodbine wild
That loves to hang, on barren boughs remote
Her wreaths of flowery perfume. These beside
Myriads, that here the Muse neglects to name,
Will add a vernal lustre to thy veil.

6 May

The Scent of Spring

From *Elizabeth and her German Garden, 1898* | Elizabeth Von Arnim (1866–1941)

This is less a garden than a wilderness. No one has lived in the house, much less in the garden, for twenty-five years, and it is such a pretty old place that the people who might have lived here and did not, deliberately preferring the horrors of a flat in a town, must have belonged to that vast number of eyeless and earless persons of whom the world seems chiefly composed. Noseless too, though it does not sound pretty; but the greater part of my spring happiness is due to the scent of the wet earth and young leaves.

7 May

A Gardening Fair at a Chateau

From *The Curious Gardener, 2010* | Anna Pavord (1940–)

Journées des Plantes de Courson:
The atmosphere is laid-back, but it is the kind of laid-back that comes from attention to detail and an enormous amount of planning. Everything works. The chateau at Courson is set in a park, laid out in a way which the French call 'le style anglais', but which isn't really English at all. They choose and place their trees quite differently from us. Around the house are courtyards and barns and cart sheds with wide parkland beyond, all enclosed by stands of magnificent horse chestnuts. During the Courson Journées, stalls are laid out in the buildings, although most are in the park, either in the open or sheltered by white canvas booths.

The first thing you notice is that the French like to buy their plants BIG. Forget plastic carrier bags. Here there are porters with trolleys to wheel sold plants from stalls to car. I watched one of them transferring a rhododendron in full flower to the car park. It was beautifully rootballed in sacking and at least 5 feet (1½ metres) high and wide. The porter eased it over the bumpy grass more carefully than if he had been pushing his grandmother.

One woman was staggering towards the car park with a climbing rose at least 12 feet (4 metres) tall, pink, in full flower, and swathed round with polythene sheeting. She looked as though she was about to toss the caber in some Highland Games, hands locked underneath the pot, face completely lost behind the bulk of the rose's stems. High over her shoulders the flowers waved to passers-by.

We can do shows very well in England. We can do plant sales too. We can certainly provide settings that might match Courson. But I haven't ever been to an event in England that had the *joie de vivre* there seemed to be at Courson. Nor such good coffee.

The Drive at Manderley

From *Rebecca, 1938* | Daphne du Maurier (1907–1989)

This drive twisted and turned as a serpent, scarce wider in
places than a path, and above our heads was a great colonnade
of trees, whose branches nodded and intermingled with one
another, making an archway for us, like the roof of a church.
Even the midday sun could not penetrate the interlacing of those
green leaves, they were too thickly entwined, one with another,
and only little flickering patches of warm light would come in
intermittent waves to dapple the drive with gold. It was very
silent, very still. On the high-road there had been a gay west
wind blowing in my face, making the grass on the hedges dance
in unison, but here there was no wind. Even the engine of the car
had taken a new note, throbbing low, quieter than before. As the
drive descended to the valley so the trees came in upon us, great
beeches with lovely smooth white stems, lifting their myriad
branches to one another, and other trees, trees I could not name,
coming close, so close that I could touch them with my hands.
On we went, over a little bridge that spanned a narrow stream,
and still this drive that was no drive twisted and turned like an
enchanted ribbon through the dark and silent woods, penetrating
even deeper to the very heart surely of the forest itself, and still
there was no clearing, no space to hold a house.

Sowing Grass Seed or a Phrenzy of Plantisede

From *Garden Rubbish, 1936* | W. C. Sellar (1898-1951) & R. J. Yeatman (1897–1968)

Sowing grass-seeds is cheaper [than *Mort d'Ancestor:* inheriting from a rich velvety ancestor or *Deed Turbary:* the luxury of laying down turves] and the children won't eat them (if they do, wait ten days, turn the little tiresomes inside out and turf them out on the lawn). But grass-sowing is so laborious that you have to be in a state of positively lovelawn frenzy before you can do it – as follows:

Dig up ground to a depth of at least 10 spits and pick out all the thin sand, clay, boulders, fossilized bowler hats, etc.; in fact remove the whole front garden and throw it away, or give it to a hospital or something. Now plant drain-pipes 3 inches apart: this will serve as a solid foundation (or don't you think so?). Fork in liberally peat-moss, pond-mud, and short stable-manure: rake over tyrannically with a rough rake and roll flat (being careful not to trip over roller and fall flat onto rough rake). Now rake absolutely flat-out with fine rake and roll flatter (say, with flat roller). Stretch strands of black cotton cats-cradically to snare sparrows, self, etc. Set slug-traps, mouse-traps, man-traps, tank-traps, and (if you are a hopeless pessimist) dig deep holes for wild elephants to fall into.

Finally, if there is still time, *remember to sow some grass-seed.* But examine it first: if it proves to have been rhododendron seed, the results will be so different – so much bigger, for instance, and so much more difficult to roll . . .

The Mower Against Gardens

Andrew Marvell (1621–1678)

Luxurious Man, to bring his Vice in use,
    Did after him the World seduce:
And from the fields the Flow'rs and Plants allure,
    Where Nature was most plain and pure.
He first enclos'd within the Gardens square
    A dead and standing pool of Air,
And a more luscious Earth for them did knead,
    Which stupifi'd them while it fed.
The Pink grew then as double as his Mind;
    The nutriment did change the kind.
With strange perfumes he did the Roses taint,
    And Flow'rs themselves were taught to paint.
The Tulip, white, did for complexion seek;
    And learn'd to interline its cheek:
Its Onion root they then so high did hold,
    That one was for a Meadow sold.
Another World was search'd, through Oceans new,
    To find the Marvel of Peru.
And yet these Rarities might be allow'd
    To Man, that sov'raign thing and proud;

Had he not dealt between the Bark and Tree,
    Forbidden mixtures there to see.
No Plant now knew the Stock from which it came;
    He grafts upon the Wild the Tame:
That the uncertain and adult'rate fruit
    Might put the Palate in dispute.
His green Seraglio has its Eunuchs too,
    Lest any Tyrant him out-doe.
And in the Cherry he does Nature vex,
    To procreate without a Sex.
'Tis all enforc'd, the Fountain and the Grot,
    While the sweet Fields do lye forgot:
Where willing Nature does to all dispense
    A wild and fragrant Innocence:
And Fauns and Faryes do the Meadows till,
    More by their presence than their skill.
Their Statues, polish'd by some ancient hand,
    May to adorn the Gardens stand:
But howsoe'er the Figures do excel,
    The Gods themselves with us do dwell.

From Balcony to Garden

From *Urban Gardener, 1999* | Elspeth Thompson (1961–2010)

12 MAY 1996

As I prepare to leave this central London shoe-box for a house
south of the river, I realise it is the balcony that I shall miss most.
This might seem odd, considering I am about to acquire my
first ever proper urban garden, but a decade of fiddling about
with pots above the rooftops has left its mark on me. Before this
I lived in a flat above a busy row of shops which had a south-
facing asphalt terrace that I filled with flowering shrubs and
bright annuals in old tin baths and fire buckets. In summer we
used to haul the furniture out through windows and sit reading
the papers while passengers on the double deckers waved at us
through a screen of sunflowers.

Since then, things have got smaller but a little smarter. At ten by
five foot, this balcony is less than a quarter the size of the terrace,
but it looks out over a tree-filled park, with a wall-to-wall view
of green leaves in high summer. It is sheltered by the balcony of
the flat above – a major advantage over a garden in bad weather
– and some of the best memories I shall take away from it are of
watching, safe and dry, as a summer storm thrashed around the
sky and sheets of rain lashed a few feet from my face. The south-
east aspect makes it a sunny spot for breakfast while the city
kick-starts itself into life below. There's nothing like a quiet perch
above it all for starting the day in a good mood.

Rhododendrons

From *Reflections at Sheffield Place, written 1937* | Virginia Woolf
(1882–1941)

The great ponds at Sheffield Place at the right season of the
year are bordered with red, white, and purple reflections for
rhododendrons are massed upon the banks and when the wind
passes over the real flowers the water flowers shake and break into
each other.

13 May

Nature's Energy

From *My Summer in a Garden, 1870* | Charles Dudley Warner
(1829–1900)

WHILE YOU ARE DECIDING WHAT TO GROW:
While you are waiting, Nature does not wait. Her mind is made
up. She knows just what she will raise; and she has an infinite
variety of early and late. The most humiliating thing to me about
a garden is the lesson it teaches of the inferiority of man. Nature
is prompt, decided, inexhaustible. She thrusts up her plants with
a vigor and freedom that I admire; and the more worthless the
plant, the more rapid and splendid its growth. She is at it early
and late, and all night; never tiring, nor showing the least sign
of exhaustion.

14 May

A Garden by the Sea

Lines 1–11 | William Morris (1834–1896)

I know a little garden-close,
Set thick with lily and red rose,
Where I would wander if I might,
From dewy morn to dewy night,
And have one with me wandering.

And though within it no birds sing,
And though no pillared house is there,
And though the apple-boughs are bare
Of fruit and blossom, would to God
Her feet upon the green grass trod,
And I beheld them as before.

The Great Wonder

From *The Well-Tempered Garden, 1970* | Christopher Lloyd
(1921–2006)

The great wonder, in gardening, is that so many plants live.

16 May

Calves Snout or Snapdragon

From *The Herball, 1597* | John Gerard (1545–1612)

The purple Snapdragon hath great and brittle stalks, which divideth it selfe into many fragile branches, whereupon do grow long leaves sharpe pointed, very greene, like unto those of wilde flax, but much greater, set by couples one opposite against another. The floures grow at the top of the stalkes, of a purple colour, fashioned like a frogs mouth, or rather a dragons mouth, from whence the women have taken the name Snapdragon. The seed is blacke, contained in round huskes fashioned like a calves snout, (whereupon some have called it Calves snout) or in mine opinion it is more like unto the bones of a sheeps head that hath beene long in the water, or the flesh consumed cleane away.

. . . .

Snapdragon is called in English, Calves snout, Snapdragon and Lyons snap: in French, *Teste de chien,* and *Teste de Veau.*

They report (saith Dioscorides) that the herbe being hanged about one preserveth a man from being bewitched, and that it maketh a man gracious in the sight of people.

The Benefits of a Cottage Garden

From *Miss Marjoribanks, 1866* | Margaret Oliphant (1828–1897)

By this time it was getting dark, and it was very pleasant in Grove
Street, where most of the good people had just watered their little
gardens, and brought out the sweetness of the mignonette. Mr
Cavendish was not sentimental, but still the hour was not without
its influence; and when he looked at the lights that began to
appear in the parlour windows, and breathed in the odours from
the little gardens, it is not to be denied that he asked himself for a
moment what was the good of going through all this bother and
vexation, and whether love in a cottage, with a little garden full
of mignonette and a tolerable amount of comfort within, was not,
after all, a great deal more reasonable than it looked at first sight?

18 May

Cottage Garden Plants

From *Cottage Garden Flowers, 1961* | Margery Fish (1892–1969)

It is difficult to know what we mean when we talk about a
cottage garden plant. It is usually something that is good-
tempered and pleasing, quite an ordinary plant that is not
particular about soil or position. Some of them are still listed in a
few nurserymen's catalogues, but by degrees they are disappearing
and most of us get our odd plants from someone else's garden.

19 May

A Sensitive Plant

From *Part I, verses 1–3* | Percy Bysshe Shelley (1792–1822)

A Sensitive Plant in a garden grew,
And the young winds fed it with silver dew,
And it opened its fan-like leaves to the light.
And closed them beneath the kisses of Night.

And the Spring arose on the garden fair,
Like the Spirit of Love felt everywhere;
And each flower and herb on Earth's dark breast
Rose from the dreams of its wintry rest.

But none ever trembled and panted with bliss
In the garden, the field, or the wilderness,
Like a doe in the noontide with love's sweet want,
As the companionless Sensitive Plant.

Time in the Medieval Books of Hours

From *The Morville Hours, 2008* | Katherine Swift (1956–)

The concept of time being sanctified by use is fundamental to
the Hours: to waste it is to waste our most precious asset, time
upon this earth. This does not mean we should be everlastingly
working in our gardens. Simply sitting and enjoying the garden
is not doing nothing; it is the attentiveness of which the Hours
speak. To watch time passing, noting the changes month by
month, day by day, hour by hour – to live, as Thoreau said,
deliberately – is a sort of sanctification in itself. It is Indifference
which is the real sin.

21 May

More Varied Beauty

From *The Wild Garden, 1870* | William Robinson (1838–1935)

My object in the *Wild Garden* is now to show how we may have
more of the varied beauty of hardy flowers than the most ardent
admirer of the old style of garden ever dreams of, by naturalising
innumerable beautiful natives of many regions of the earth in
our woods and copses, rougher parts of pleasure grounds, and in
unoccupied places in almost every kind of garden.

I allude not to the wood and brake flora of any one country,
but to that which finds its home in the vast fields of the whole
northern world, and that of the hill-ground that falls in furrowed
folds from beneath the hoary heads of all the great mountain
chains of the world, whether they rise from hot Indian plains or
green European pastures.

22 May

Fine Advice, Not Taken

From *Kit and Kitty, 1890* | R. D. Blackmore (1825–1900)

ONE COLD MAY MORNING:

My uncle used to read the gardening papers; which always bloom with fine advice; and one of them had lately been telling largely how, in Continental vineyards, these cold freaks of heaven are met by the sacrificial smoke of earth. To wit, a hundred pyres are raised of the rakings and refuse of the long vine-alleys, and ready for kindling on the frosty verge. Then a wisp of lighted straw is applied to each, when the sparkling shafts of frost impend, and a genial smoke is wafted through, and Sagittarius has his eyes obscured. I told my uncle that this was rubbish, at least as regarded our level lands; though it might be of service upon a hillside. That if there were wind enough to spread the smoke, there must also be enough to prevent the hoar-frost, which alone need be feared at this season. But he told me to stick to what I understood; for these scientific things were beyond me, and my business was to tend the fires.

But in spite of all this brave talk, he was afraid of casting a slur upon his old experience by a new experiment. For the British workman disdains new ideas, and there was not a man upon our place but would say that the governor was turned cranky, if he got any inkling of this strange scheme.

Irish Gardens

From *A letter to Harold Acton, 24 May 1965* | Nancy Mitford
(1904–1973)

Irish gardens beat all for horror. With 19 gardeners, Lord Talbot of Malahide has produced an affair exactly like a suburban golf course.

The Chelsea Flower Show

From *Garden Notebook, 1988* | Beth Chatto (1923–2018)

As we cross Chelsea Bridge I see the familiar blue and white striped canvas of some of the marquees and my heart gives sudden jumps of apprehension and anticipation. So far, despite the winter's worries, our plants look satisfactory, but the last phase of this adventure, the staging, is still, for me, the unknown element. The principles behind my planning remain the same, but each year the plants behave differently and I, too, have changed, so the combinations are never the same.

But always the same is the pleasure we have as we enter the great marquee and find some of our old friends already there. The feeling between plantspeople is genuine. You may not see someone for a year – or several years – but the feeling of kindred spirit remains. It is very heartwarming.

25 May

Planting by the Moon

From *Anne of Avonlea, 1909* | L. M. Montgomery (1874–1942)

'Ain't it an awful nice-smelling evening?' asked Davy, sniffing delightedly as he swung a hoe in his grimy hands. He had been working in his garden. That spring Marilla, by way of turning Davy's passion for revelling in mud and clay into useful channels, had given him and Dora a small plot of ground for a garden. Both had eagerly gone to work in a characteristic fashion. Dora planted, weeded, and watered carefully, systematically, and dispassionately. As a result, her plot was already green with prim, orderly little rows of vegetables and annuals. Davy, however, worked with more zeal than discretion; he dug and hoed and raked and watered and transplanted so energetically that his seeds had no chance for their lives.

'How is your garden coming on, Davy-boy?' asked Anne.

'Kind of slow,' said Davy with a sigh. 'I don't know why the things don't grow better. Milty Boulter says I must have planted them in the dark of the moon and that's the whole trouble. He says you must never sow seeds or kill pork or cut your hair or do any 'portant thing in the wrong time of the moon. Is that true, Anne? I want to know.'

'Maybe if you didn't pull your plants up by the roots every other day to see how they're getting on "at the other end," they'd do better,' said Marilla sarcastically.

'I only pulled six of them up,' protested Davy. 'I wanted to see if there was grubs at the roots. Milty Boulter said if it wasn't the moon's fault it must be grubs. But I only found one grub. He was a great big juicy curly grub. I put him on a stone and got another stone and smashed him flat. He made a jolly squash I tell you. I was sorry there wasn't more of them. Dora's garden was planted same time's mine and her things are growing all right. It *can't* be the moon,' Davy concluded in a reflective tone.

To be done in the Parterre and Flower Garden: Transplanting

From *Kalendarium Hortense, 1664* | John Evelyn (1620–1706)

Now forasmuch as *Gentlemen* are very inquisitive when were
the best and securest Seasons for exposing their *Orange-trees,*
and more tender *Curiosities,* I give them this for a Rule the most
infallible: That they observe the *Mulberry-tree,* when it begins to
put forth and open the Leaves (be it earlier or later), bring your
Oranges, &c. boldly out of the *Conservatory;* 'tis your only *Season*
to *Transplant* and *Remove* them. Let this be done with care, if
the Tree be too ponderous to be lifted *perpendicular* by the Hand
alone, by applying a *Triangle* and *Pully,* and so with a *Rope,* and
a broad *Horse-girth* at the end, lapped about the Stem (to prevent
galling) draw out the Tree, with competent Mould adhering to it,
having before loosned it from the sides of the *Case,* and so with
ease transfer it into another.

27 May

A Good Thermometer

From *The Gardener's Manual containing Practical Instructions for the Cultivation and Management of the Flower, the Fruit and the Kitchen Garden: Hot House, Green House and Conservatory. Adapted to Small or Large Gardens, eighth edition, 1843* | Anon

In May, when the weather is moderately warm and settled, you may begin to remove the most hardy green-house plants into the open air. The mulberry tree is a good thermometer on this occasion, for when that puts on its green coat, the season will admit you safely to place out green-house plants; but you cannot depend on the weather being sufficiently mild for this, before the last week in May.

28 May

Parrot Tulips

From *In Your Garden, 1951* | Vita Sackville-West (1892–1962)

FROM AN ARTICLE IN *THE OBSERVER*, MAY 29, 1949:
The Parrot or Dragon tulips are well named, for some of them really do suggest the more gaudy macaws in their colouring, and the jagged edges of their petals always remind me of the wyvern, that winged heraldic cousin of the dragon. I tried this comparison on a gardening friend, who stared at me blankly and said she couldn't think what I meant, and what was a wyvern anyhow? But I still think that one should look at flowers in an imaginative way, to squeeze the fullest enjoyment from them.

The pink *Fantasy,* with its apple-green feathering, is fairly common; *Red Champion* is a deeper version of *Fantasy,* a real cherry-red, opening to an enormous size, and heavily fringed; *Orange Favourite,* smudged with buttercup yellow and green, not quite so large; the *Blue Parrot,* which is not blue at all but a deep mauve, really the colour of blackberry fool (horticulturalists sometimes have very queer ideas about naming colours); *Sunshine,* a golden yellow – all these are fun to grow, and no more expensive to buy than the ordinary tulip.

But there are other far more frenzied variations. *Gadelan* was the maddest tulip I ever had in my garden. It was smeared with as many colours as a painter's palette after a good day's work – dark blue, dark red, purple, green, white – and as to size, it must have measured eight inches across when fully opened. This cost 1s. 3d. a bulb, so I got only three as an experiment, and abstained altogether from the *Black Parrot* at a guinea. *Gadelan* was enough, for the moment, to keep me satisfied and startled.

'Parrotting,' as it is called, is due to genetic change, i.e. a kind of sporting. It is not a disease.

29 May

To a Bed of Tulips

Robert Herrick (1591–1674)

Bright Tulips, we do know,
You had your comming hither;
And Fading-time do's show,
That Ye must quickly wither.

Your *Sister-hoods* may stay,
And smile here for your houre;
But dye ye must away:
Even as the meanest Flower.

Come Virgins then, and see
Your frailties; and bemone ye;
For lost like these, 'twill be,
As Time had never known ye.

Un Giardino Segreto

From *Mapp and Lucia, 1931* | E. F. Benson (1867–1940)

'My little plot,' said Miss Mapp. 'Very modest, as you see, three-quarters of an acre at the most, but well screened. My flower-beds: sweet roses, tortoiseshell butterflies. My Little Eden I call it, so small, but so well beloved.'

'Enchanting!' said Lucia, looking round the garden before mounting the steps to the garden-room door. There was a very green and well-kept lawn, set in bright flower beds. A trellis at one end separated it from a kitchen-garden beyond, and round the rest ran high brick walls, over which peered the roofs of other houses. In one of these walls was cut a curved archway with a della Robbia head above it.

'Shall we just pop across the lawn,' said Miss Mapp, pointing to this, 'and peep in there while Withers brings our tea? Just to stretch the – the limbs, Mrs Lucas, after your long drive. There's a wee plot beyond there which is quite a pet of mine.'

. . . .

'My little secret garden,' continued Miss Mapp as they came to the archway. 'When I am in here and shut the door, I mustn't be disturbed for anything less than a telegram. A rule of the house: I am very strict about it. The tower of the church keeping watch, as I always say over my little nook, and taking care of me. Otherwise not overlooked at all. A little paved walk round it, you see, flower-beds, a pocket-handkerchief of a lawn, and in the middle a pillar with a bust of good Queen Anne. Picked up in a shop here for a song. One of my lucky days.'

'Oh Georgie, isn't it too sweet?' cried Lucia. 'Un giardino segreto. Molto bello!'

Miss Mapp gave a little purr of ecstasy.

'How lovely to be able to talk Italian like that.' she said. 'So pleased you like my little . . . giardino segreto, was it?'

JUNE

The Early Summer Silence

A Floral Screen

From *Urban Gardener, 1999* | Elspeth Thompson (1961–2010)

1 JUNE 1997 – HOME

My idea was this: to combine an attractive plant-covered façade with a sort of floral screen for the sitting room, whose wide bay window, only a yard or two from the street, is a magnet for Nosy Parkers. If I grew tall or climbing things in the window boxes, and trailing plants in the jumble of pots on the flat, asphalted roof of the bay, I should have a display which fulfilled many purposes at once. Morning glory and nasturtiums are the plants I chose – both for their ease of cultivation and for the glorious combination of the former's clear, bright, perfect summer's-day blue with the latter's unpredictable rich tones of orange, red and saffron yellow. The climbing variety – the triffid of the nasturtium word, which I've known to reach twelve feet or more – is the one to go for. Last year's crop in our back garden covered a sunny wall with foliage and blooms right up to the first frosts just before Christmas.

Thyrsis

1865 | Matthew Arnold (1822–1888)

Verses 6 and 7

So, some tempestuous morn in early June,
    When the year's primal burst of bloom is o'er,
        Before the roses and the longest day –
When garden-walks and all the grassy floor
    With blossoms red and white of fallen May
        And chestnut-flowers are strewn –
So have I heard the cuckoo's parting cry,
    From the wet field, through the vext garden-trees,
    Come with the volleying rain and tossing breeze:
The bloom is gone, and with the bloom go I!

Too quick despairer, wherefore wilt thou go?
    Soon will the high Midsummer pomps come on,
        Soon will the musk carnations break and swell,
Soon shall we have gold-dusted snapdragon,
    Sweet-William with his homely cottage-smell,
        And stocks in fragrant blow;
Roses that down the alleys shine afar,
    And open, jasmine-muffled lattices,
    And groups under the dreaming garden-trees,
And the full moon, and the white evening-star.

The Sounds of Summer

From *Wives and Daughters, 1864–1866* | Elizabeth Gaskell
(1810–1865)

The deliciousness of the early summer silence was only broken by
the song of the birds, and the nearer hum of bees.

3 June

The Physick Garden at Corpus Christi College, Oxford

From *Through England on a Side Saddle, 1684–1703, first published 1888* | Celia Fiennes (1662–1741)

The Physick garden afforded great diversion and pleasure, the variety of flowers and plants would have entertained one a week. The few remarkable things I tooke notice off was the Aloes plant which is like a great flag in shape, leaves and Coullour, and grows in the fform of an open Hartichoake and towards the bottom of each Leafe its very broad and thicke, In which there are hollows or receptacles for the Aloes.

There is also the sensible plant, take but a Leafe between finger and thumb and squeeze it and it immediately Curles up together as if pained and after some tyme opens abroad again, it looks in Coullour like a filbert Leafe but much narrower and long. There is also the humble plant that grows on a long slender Stalke and do but strike it, it falls flatt on the ground stalke and all, and after some tyme revives againe and Stands up, but these are nice plants and are kept mostly under Glass's, the aire being too rough for them.

4 June

An Important Visitor

From *Gardens of Celebrities and Celebrated Gardens in and Around London, 1918* | Jessie Macgregor (1847–1919)

The Chelsea Physicke Garden, 1733:

The fame of the Chelsea garden was now so great that it sufficed to draw Linnæus thither. He only visited two botanic gardens in this country – that of Oxford under Professor Dillenius, and that at Chelsea. To those in control at Chelsea he often refers in very commendatory terms; and commendation from Linnæus was well worth having for his researches and writings effected a scientific revolution in all the botanic gardens of the educated world.

Satiny Poppies

From *The Secret Garden, 1911* | Frances Hodgson Burnett (1849–1924)

The seeds Dickon and Mary had planted grew as if fairies had
tended them. Satiny poppies of all tints danced in the breeze by
the score, gaily defying flowers which had lived in the garden for
years and which it might be confessed seemed rather to wonder
how such new people had got there. And the roses – the roses!
Rising out of the grass, tangled round the sun-dial, wreathing
the tree trunks and hanging from their branches, climbing up
the walls and spreading over them with long garlands falling
in cascades – they came alive day by day, hour by hour. Fair
fresh leaves, and buds – and buds – tiny at first but swelling and
working Magic until they burst and uncurled into cups of scent
delicately spilling themselves over their brims and filling the
garden air.

6 June

The Garden-Patch

From *Uncle Tom's Cabin, 1852* | Harriet Beecher Stowe (1811–1896)

In front it had a neat garden-patch, where, every summer,
strawberries, raspberries, and a variety of fruits and vegetables,
flourished under careful tending. The whole front of it was
covered by a large scarlet bignonia and a native multiflora rose,
which, entwisting and interlacing, left scarce a vestige of the
rough logs to be seen. Here, also, in summer, various brilliant
annuals, such as marigolds, petunias, four-o'clocks, found an
indulgent corner in which to unfold their splendors, and were
the delight and pride of Aunt Chloe's heart.

7 June

Seats and Banks of Camomile

From *A New Orchard and Garden, 1618* | William Lawson
(c.1554–1635)

Large walks, broad and long, close and open, like the Tempe
Groves in Thessalie, raised with gravell and sand, having seats and
banks of Camomile, all this delights the minde and brings health
to the body.

8 June

Eutopia

Francis Turner Palgrave (1824–1897)

There is a garden where lilies
    And roses are side by side;
And all day between them in silence
    The silken butterflies glide.

I may not enter the garden,
    Though I know the road thereto;
And morn by morn to the gateway
    I see the children go.

They bring back light on their faces;
    But they cannot bring back to me
What the lilies say to the roses,
    Or the songs of the butterflies be.

Biennials

From *Green Thoughts, 1981* | Eleanor Perényi (1918–2009)

In the golden age when a flower garden was looked at as a kind
of stage, biennials were important to the *mise-en-scène* of the
herbaceous border. Canterbury bells like ruffled pagodas, sweet
Williams and wallflowers, each with its distinctive perfume,
bannered armies of foxgloves – these were the principals. They
bloom in June after the bulbs are over and midsummer perennials
are still in the wings, an interlude that needs filling. But their
day may be over. Biennials bloom for about a month (Canterbury
bells a little longer if the first flush of blooms is plucked, allowing
a second to take its place), then die. And to achieve this brief
performance they must be started from seed a year before, then
thinned out and reset in winter either in the seed bed or the
border where they are to flower – in New England, the former is
best – and they should be transplanted in early spring. They are
rarely to be had ready-made. Few garden centers carry them, and
those that do put them on sale too late, towards the end of May,
as half-grown plants. A biennial by then should be full size and
about to flower or it will be a poor thing in the garden. So there
is really no alternative to raising them yourself if you want them.

I sometimes think I don't. There have been years when I was
ill, absent, or lazy and didn't sow the seed. I always regretted it.
Nothing quite takes the place of biennials, even if those places are
empty by July.

The Rosery

From *The Moonstone, 1868* | Wilkie Collins (1824–1889)

SERGEANT CUFF'S LONG-TERM PLANS:
Sergeant Cuff looked through the evergreen arch on our left,
spied out our rosery, and walked straight in, with the first
appearance of anything like interest that he had shown yet. To
the gardener's astonishment, and to my disgust, this celebrated
policeman proved to be quite a mine of learning on the trumpery
subject of rose-gardens.

'Ah, you've got the right exposure here to the south and sou'-
west,' says the Sergeant, with a wag of his grizzled head, and a
streak of pleasure in his melancholy voice. 'This is the shape for
a rosary — nothing like a circle set in a square. Yes, yes; with
walks between all the beds. But they oughtn't to be gravel walks
like these. Grass, Mr Gardener — grass walks between your roses;
gravel's too hard for them. That's a sweet pretty bed of white
roses and blush roses. They always mix well together, don't they?
Here's the white musk rose, Mr Betteredge — our old English rose
holding up its head along with the best and the newest of them.

Pretty dear!' says the Sergeant, fondling the Musk Rose with his lanky fingers, and speaking to it as if he was speaking to a child.

This was a nice sort of man to recover Miss Rachel's Diamond, and to find out the thief who stole it!

'You seem to be fond of roses, Sergeant?' I remarked.

'I haven't much time to be fond of anything,' says Sergeant Cuff. 'But when I have a moment's fondness to bestow, most times, Mr Betteredge, the roses get it. I began my life among them in my father's nursery garden, and I shall end my life among them, if I can. Yes. One of these days (please God) I shall retire from catching thieves, and try my hand at growing roses. There will be grass walks, Mr Gardener, between my beds,' says the Sergeant, on whose mind the gravel paths of our rosery seemed to dwell unpleasantly.

Charming Names

From *Home and Garden, 1900* | Gertrude Jekyll (1843–1932)

Nobody now says Gillyflower, though it is a much better name than the vague Carnation; and the pretty Eglantine, though the sound of it is still known, is put away in the lumber-room of things not used or wanted; and most people have even forgotten that it was the older name for Sweet-brier. And as for all that rollicking company of Bobbing Joan and Blooming Sally and Bouncing Bet, they have long been lost, reappearing only in the dull but more decorous guise of Wild Arum and French Willow and Soapwort.

But let us treasure the best of our old plant-names, Sweet Sultan and Bachelors' Buttons, Eyebright, Foxglove, Nightshade and London Pride, and especially those that have about them a flavour of poetical feeling or old country romance, such as Travellers' Joy, Meadowsweet, Speedwell, Forget-me-not, Lads'-love, Sweet Cicely, Love-in-a-mist.

The Sunlight on the Garden

Written *1936, published 1937* | Louis MacNeice (1907–1963)

The sunlight on the garden
Hardens and grows cold,
We cannot cage the minute
Within its nets of gold,
When all is told
We cannot beg for pardon.

Our freedom as free lances
Advances towards its end;
The earth compels, upon it
Sonnets and birds descend;
And soon, my friend,
We shall have no time for dances.

The sky was good for flying
Defying the church bells
And every evil iron
Siren and what it tells:
The earth compels,
We are dying, Egypt, dying

And not expecting pardon,
Hardened in heart anew,
But glad to have sat under
Thunder and rain with you,
And grateful too
For sunlight on the garden.

To be done in the Parterre and Flower Garden: Saving and Sowing

From *Kalendarium Hortense, 1664* | John Evelyn (1620–1706)

Transplant *Autumnal Cyclamens* now, if you would change their place; otherwise let them stand.

Gather the ripe *Seeds of Flowers* worth the saving, as of choicest *Oriental Jacinth, Narcissus* (the two lesser, pale, spurious *Daffodils,* of a whitish green, often produces Varieties), *Auriculas, Ranunculus's,* &c. and preserve them dry: Shade your *Carnations* from the Afternoon Sun.

You may now begin to lay your *Gilly-flowers.* Sow some *Annuals* to flower in the later Months.

Take up your *Tulips Bulbs,* burying such immediately as you find naked upon your *Beds*, or else *plant* them in some *cooler* place, and *refresh* over-parch'd *Beds* with Water.

14 June

The Gardens at Vauxhall

From *Vanity Fair, 1848* | William Makepeace Thackeray (1811–1863)

THE DELIGHTS OF THE GARDENS:

The hundred thousand *extra* lamps, which were always lighted;
the fiddlers in cocked-hats, who played ravishing melodies under
the gilded cockle-shell in the midst of the Gardens; the singers,
both of comic and sentimental ballads, who charmed the ears
there; the country dances, formed by bouncing cockneys and
cockneyesses, and executed amidst jumping, thumping and
laughter; the signal which announced that Madame Saqui was
about to mount skyward on a slack rope ascending to the stars;
the hermit that always sat in the illuminated hermitage; the dark
walks, so favourable to the interviews of young lovers; the pots of
stout handed about by the people in the shabby old liveries; and
the twinkling boxes, in which the happy feasters made-believe to
eat slices of almost invisible ham.

15 June

199

The Mulberry Garden

From *The Pleasure Garden, 1976* | Leon Garfield (1921–1996)

Eastward in Clerkenwell lies the Mulberry Pleasure Garden: six
acres of leafy walks, colonnades, pavilions and arbours of box,
briar and vine, walled in between Rag Street and New Prison
Walk. When night falls, the garden opens its eyes; lamps hang
glimmering in the trees and scores of moths flap and totter in the
shadowy green, imagining themselves star-drunk.

16 June

Old-Fashioned Flowers

From *The Book of Old-Fashioned Flowers, 1901* | Harry Roberts
(1871–1946)

Strictly, of course, the term is indefinite, for old-fashioned flowers
and old-fashioned gardens mean to different people different
things. Probably to most people — at all events to the present
writer — old-fashioned gardening means that system which is in
direct opposition to prim geometric beds and to the imitation of
carpet patterns by arrangement of flowers.

. . . .

The greatest joy which a garden can yield is a feeling of
restfulness and peace, a feeling which no garden of staring beds
and ostentatious splendour can afford, but which is yielded — as
by nothing else in the world — by a garden of happy, homely, old-
fashioned flowers.

17 June

The Old Pinks

From *Cottage Garden Flowers, 1961* | Margery Fish (1892–1969)

Whenever we think of an old-world garden we think of pinks.
Gillyflowers, they were called in the old days, or 'sweet Johns',
and they belong, more than any other flower, to the days of sun-
bonnets and print gowns and the little crowded gardens of the past.

Straw-berries

From *The Herball, 1597* | John Gerard (1545–1612)

There be divers sorts of Straw-berries; one red, another white, a third sort greene, and likewise a wilde Straw-berry, which is altogether barren of fruit.

The fruit or berries are called in *Latine* by *Virgil* and *Ovid, Fraga:* neither have they any other name commonly knowne: in French *Fraises:* in English, Straw-berries.

The leaves boyled and applied in manner of a pultis taketh away the burning heate in wounds: the decoction thereof strengthneth the gummes, fastneth the teeth.

The distilled water drunke with white Wine is good against the passion of the heart, reviving the spirits, and making the heart merry.

The ripe Straw-berries quence thirst, and take away, if they be often used, the rednesse and heate of the face.

Sonnet to Diana

Sonnet ii | Henry Constable (1562–1613)

My lady's presence makes the roses red,
Because they see her lips they blush with shame.
   The lily's leaves for envy pale became,
And her white hands in them this envy bred.
The marigold the leaves abroad did spread,
   Because the sun's and her power is the same.
   The violet of purple colour came,
Dyed in the blood she made my heart to shed.
In brief, all flowers from her their virtue take;
   From her sweet breath their sweet smells do proceed;
The living heat, which her eyebeams do make,
   Warmeth the ground and quickeneth the seed.
     The rain, wherein she watereth the flowers,
     Falls from mine eyes which she dissolves in showers.

Mulberries and Silk

From *Instructions in Gardening for Ladies, 1840* | Jane Loudon
(1807–1858)

There are three distinct species of mulberry, besides innumerable
varieties. The distinct species are the white, only used for feeding
silk-worms with its leaves; the black, which is generally grown
in gardens for its fruit; and the red, or American mulberry. Many
persons are not aware of the difference between the black and
the white mulberries, and they think that if they have a mulberry
tree in their garden, they cannot do better than feed their silk-
worms with its leaves; though the fact is that the white mulberry
is scarcely ever grown in England, and the leaves of the black
mulberry are positively injurious to the worms. Lettuce leaves
are indeed better than any other food for silk-worms reared in
England. The fruit of the red mulberry is eatable, but not very
good; and its leaves are injurious to silkworms.

21 June

In the Conservatory

From *The Mill on the Floss, 1860* | George Eliot (1819–1880)

'How strange and unreal the trees and flowers look with the lights among them,' said Maggie, in a low voice. 'They look as if they belonged to an enchanted land, and would never fade away – I could fancy they were all made of jewels.'

Excellence

From *A Love of Flowers, 1971* | H. E. Bates (1905–1974)

I call a plant excellent when it has the following virtues: that of being able to stand on its own legs without stakes, of producing flowers of great beauty for weeks on end and of showing incontestable grace of form.

The Garden

From *Edward Fitzgerald's translation of The Rubáiyát of Omar Khayyám, 1859* | Omar ibn Ibrahim al-Khayyám (1048–1131) | Edward Fitzgerald (1809–1883)

XVIII

I sometimes think that never blows so red
The Rose as where some buried Cæsar bled;
    That every Hyacinth the Garden wears
Dropt in its Lap from some once lovely Head.

XIX

And this delightful Herb whose tender Green
Fledges the River's Lip on which we lean –
    Ah, lean upon it lightly! for who knows
From what once lovely Lip it springs unseen!

Scrumping an Orange

From *The Diary of Samuel Pepys, 1666* | Samuel Pepys (1633–1703)

25TH JUNE 1666

Mrs Pen carried us to two gardens at Hackney, which I every day
grow more and more in love with, Mr Drake's one, where the
garden is good, and house and the prospect admirable; the other
my Lord Brooke's, where the gardens are much better, but the
house not so good, nor the prospect good at all. But the gardens
are excellent and here I first saw oranges grow: some green, some
half, some a quarter, and some full ripe, on the same tree; and
one fruit of the same tree do come a year or two after the other. I
pulled off a little one by stealth, the man being mightily curious
of them, and ate it, and it was just as other little green small
oranges are; as big as half the end of my little finger. Here were
also great variety of other exotic plants, and several labyrinths,
and a pretty aviary.

25 June

The Vegetable or Kitchen Garden: A Balancing Act

From *The Beeton Book of Garden Management, 1862* | Samuel Orchart Beeton (1831–1877)

Many principal crops come in this month, and, following suddenly upon a time when the supply from the kitchen-garden is somewhat scanty, show the real effect of cropping too abundantly in the early part of the year. Peas, beans, cauliflowers, carrots, potatoes, and many other vegetables, come in all at once, that could not be produced earlier in the open ground. All show the propriety of dispersing the crops more regularly through the season.

The young gardener should make a note of it, and endeavour to manage so that there is no flush of vegetables at one time and a dearth of them at others. Particularly let it be borne in mind that we have long cold springs, in which the weather is exceedingly variable and mostly ungenial, when vegetation makes very slow progress indeed; it is then that root-crops and Brassicæ come in so useful; then that Brussels sprouts, kale, and broccoli, yield a succession of sweet wholesome sprouts, that grow almost in the coldest weather, and form the principal supply from Christmas to May. It is now the time to look forward to that time and be well prepared for it, so that available space should have been left, in which a plentiful supply of the above-named can be grown. Ground that has been lying fallow since the winter can now be turned to good account; and be it remembered that fifty firm stocky plants of broccoli will yield a better supply than a hundred plants that have been drawn up between other crops, or been crowded.

Mrs Lambert's Garden Hat

From *The Real Charlotte, 1894* Somerville & Ross | E. Œ. / Edith
Somerville (1858–1949) & Martin Ross / Violet Florence Martin (1862–1915)

She still, as she had always done, bought her expensive Sunday
bonnet as she would have bought a piece of furniture, because
it was handsome, not because it was becoming. The garden
hat which she now wore could not pretend to either of these
qualifications.

27 June

Gardening in Britain

From *An Encyclopaedia of Gardening, 1822* | John Claudius Loudon
(1783–1843)

From the number of Roman villas, which antiquaries, from time
to time, discover to have existed in Britain; and especially from
the extent of some that have been recently disinterred, there can
be little doubt that the Romans introduced their gardening in
this country.

The First Crop

From *The Juvenile Gardener, 1824* | Written by a Lady for the use of her own Children, with a view to giving them an early taste for the Pleasures of a Garden and the Study of Botany.

FRANK AND AGNES VERNON, AGED 6 AND 4 RESPECTIVELY:
The month of June was drawing to a close, when, one day, Frank entered his mother's dressing-room with a cabbage-leaf in his hand, which contained a few strawberries, the first produce of the plants in his garden, which he had watched with great anxiety for several days, that he might give them to his mamma, who was much pleased with his attention.

As Frank did not show the least wish to take any himself, Mrs Vernon told him and Agnes to eat some; and they both thought them the most delicious fruit they had ever eaten: so much satisfaction do we derive from that which has called forth our industry and exertion.

29 June

The Flower's Name

Robert Browning (1812–1889)

Here's the garden she walked across,
    Arm in my arm, such a short while since;
Hark, now I push its wicket, the moss
    Hinders the hinges and makes them wince!
She must have reached this shrub ere she turned,
    As back with that murmur the wicket swung;
For she laid the poor snail, my chance foot spurned,
    To feed and forget it the leaves among.

Down this side of the gravel-walk
    She went while her robe's edge brushed the box;
And here she paused in her gracious talk
    To point me a moth on the milk-white phlox.
Roses, ranged in valiant row,
    I will never think that she passed you by!
She loves you, noble roses, I know;
    But yonder, see, where the rock-plants lie!

This flower she stopped at, finger on lip,
    Stooped over, in doubt, as settling its claim;
Till she gave me, with pride to make no slip,
    Its soft meandering Spanish name.
What a name! Was it love or praise?
    Speech half-asleep or song half-awake?
I must learn Spanish, one of these days,
    Only for that slow sweet name's sake.

Roses, if I live and do well,
    I may bring her, one of these days,
To fix you fast with as fine a spell,
    Fit you each with his Spanish phrase;
But do not detain me now; for she lingers
    There, like sunshine over the ground,
And ever I see her soft white fingers
    Searching after the bud she found.

Flower, you Spaniard, look that you grow not;
    Stay as you are and be loved for ever!
Bud, if I kiss you 'tis that you blow not;
    Mind, the shut pink mouth opens never!
For while it pouts, her fingers wrestle,
    Twinkling the audacious leaves between,
Till round they turn and down they nestle –
    Is not the dear mark still to be seen?

Where I find her not, beauties vanish;
    Whither I follow her, beauties flee;
Is there no method to tell her in Spanish
    June's twice June since she breathed it with me?
Come, bud, show me the least of her traces,
    Treasure my lady's lightest footfall
– Ah, you may flout and turn up your faces –
    Roses, you are not so fair after all!

JULY

Petals Stirred by a Summer Breeze

Flower Arrangements

From *Rustic Adornments for Homes of Taste, 1856* | Shirley
Hibberd (1825–1890)

It would be a rather difficult matter to sum up all the social
qualities of flowers. Do we not always feel welcome when, on
entering a room, we find a display of flowers on the table? Where
there are flowers about, does not the hostess appears glad, the
children pleased, the very parrot garrulous, at our arrival; the
whole scene and all the personages more hearty, homely, and
beautiful, because of those bewitching roses, and brugmansias,
and pavonias, and mignionette! Assuredly, of all simple domestic
ornaments flowers must have the first place.

1 July

Alstroemerias

From *In Your Garden, 1951* | Vita Sackville-West (1892–1962)

FROM AN ARTICLE IN *THE OBSERVER,* JULY 2, 1950:
There are some moments when I feel pleased with my garden,
and other moments when I despair. The pleased moments usually
happen in spring, and last up to the middle of June. By that time
all the freshness has gone off; everything has become heavy;
everything has lost that adolescent look, that look of astonishment
at its own youth. The middle-aged spread has begun.

It is then that the *Alstroemerias* come into their own. Lumps
of colour . . . I have mentioned them before, I know, but a
reminder will do no harm. They are in flower now, so this is the
opportunity to go and see them, either in a local nurseryman's
plot, or in a private garden, or at a flower show. The yellow
Peruvian lily, A. *aurantiaca,* was and is a common sight in cottage
gardens and old herbaceous borders, where it was regarded almost
as a weed, but it has been superseded by the far more beautiful
Ligtu hybrids, in varied colours of coral and buff, and by A.
haemantha, a brilliant orange. (Keep the orange away from the
coral, for they do not mix well together, and whoever it was
said Nature made no mistakes in colour-harmony was either
colour-blind or a sentimentalist. Nature sometimes makes the
most hideous mistakes; and it is up to us gardeners to control and
correct them.)

2 July

A Shakespearian Garden

From *Queen Lucia, 1920* | E. F. Benson (1867–1940)

3 July

THE HOUSE STOOD AT THE END OF THE VILLAGE:
A yew-hedge bought entire from a neighbouring farm, and
transplanted with solid lumps of earth and indignant snails about
its roots, separated the small oblong garden from the road, and
cast monstrous shadows of the shapes into which it was cut, across
the little lawn inside. Here, as was only right and proper, there
was not a flower to be found save such as were mentioned in the
plays of Shakespeare: indeed, it was called Shakespeare's garden,
and the bed that ran below the windows of the dining-room was
Ophelia's border for it consisted solely of those flowers which
that distraught maiden distributed to her friends when she should
have been in a lunatic asylum. Mrs Lucas often reflected how
lucky it was that such institutions were unknown in Elizabeth's
day. Pansies, naturally, formed the chief decoration (though
there were some very flourishing plants of rue), and Mrs Lucas
always wore a little bunch of them when in flower, to inspire
her thoughts, and found them wonderfully efficacious. Round
the sundial, which was set in the middle of one of the squares of
grass between which a path of broken paving stones led to the
front-door, was a circular border, now, in July, sadly vacant, for
it harboured only the spring flowers enumerated by Perdita. But
the first day every year when Perdita's border put forth its earliest
blossom was a delicious anniversary, and the news of it spread
like wildfire through Mrs Lucas's kingdom, and her subjects were
very joyful, and came to salute the violet or daffodil, or whatever
it was.

Rosemary for Remembrance

From *Hamlet, dated c.1600, registered for publication 1602*

William Shakespeare (1564–1616)

ACT IV, SCENE V

Ophelia
There's rosemary, that's for remembrance; pray,
love, remember. And there is pansies; that's for thoughts.

. . . .

There's fennel for you, and columbines. There's
rue for you, and here's some for me. We may call it
herb-grace o' Sundays. O, you must wear your rue
with a difference. There's a daisy. I would give you
some violets, but they withered all when my father
died. They say he made a good end.

4 July

An Unfortunate Notice

From *Domestic Manners of the Americans, 1832* | Fanny Trollope
(1779–1863)

At Cincinnati there is a garden where the people go to eat ices, and to look at roses. For the preservation of the flowers, there is placed at the end of one of the walks a sign-post sort of daub, representing a Swiss peasant girl, holding in her hand a scroll, requesting that the roses might not be gathered. Unhappily for the artist, or for the proprietor, or for both, the petticoat of this figure was so short as to shew her ancles. The ladies saw, and shuddered; and it was formally intimated to the proprietor, that if he wished for the patronage of the ladies of Cincinnati, he must have the petticoat of this figure lengthened. The affrighted purveyor of ices sent off an express for the artist and his paint pot. He came, but unluckily not provided with any colour that would match the petticoat; the necessity, however, was too urgent for delay, and a flounce of blue was added to the petticoat of red, giving bright and shining evidence before all men of the immaculate delicacy of the Cincinnati ladies.

On a Sun-Dial

From *Sketches and Essays, 1839* | William Hazlitt (1778–1830)

Horas non numero nisi serenas – is the motto of a sun-dial near
Venice. There is a softness and a harmony in the words and in the
thought unparalleled. Of all conceits it is surely the most classical.
'I count only the hours that are serene.' What a bland and care-
dispelling feeling! How the shadows seem to fade on the dial-
plate as the sky lours, and time presents only a blank unless as
its progress is marked by what is joyous and all that is not happy
sinks into oblivion!

6 July

223

The Sundial

Verses 1 and 2 | Austin Dobson (1840–1921)

'Tis an old dial, dark with many a stain;
   In summer crowned with drifting orchard bloom,
Tricked in the autumn with the yellow rain,
   And white in winter like a marble tomb;

Round about its gray, time-eaten brow
   Lean letters speak – a worn and shattered row
I am a Shade: a Shadowe too arte thou:
   I marke the Time: saye, Gossip, dost thou soe?

To Grow Long and Tender Cucumbers

From *The Gardener's Labyrinth, 1577* | Thomas Hill (c.1528–1574)

The Gardener myndyng to possesse long and tender Cucumbers, ought to sette under the young fruites growyng, an Earthen Panne, Bole, or halfe Tubbe, fylled with fayre water, wel five or six fyngers, yea, halfe a foote distance from them, for these by the nexte day, will bee stretched unto the water, so that settyng the Pannes lower into the Earth, or raysyng the fruites higher, ye shall daylye see them stretched forth towardes the water, unto the admiration of the owner, for the length of them, which deprived of their vessels of water, shall in a contrarie manner see them wynded and crooking, so muche these joye in the moysture, and hate the drouth. The fruites likewise will grow of a marvellous length, if the flowres be put to grow wythin hollowe Canes or Pypes of Elder.

But the same is otherwise to be learned of the Oyle, for as the Cucumbers so deadly hate (as *Plinie writeth*) by setting vessels of the oyle, in steed of the water under them, they after bend and wynde away, as disdaining the Licour, whych the owner shall wel try and see that these to have bended so crooked or winding as an hooke in one nights space.

A Pink Bedroom

From *The Elf of the Rose, 1839* | Hans Christian Andersen (1805-1875) | Translated by M. R. James (1862–1936)

In the middle of a garden there grew a rose tree which was quite full of blossoms, and in one of these, the prettiest of them all, lived an Elf: he was such a little tiny thing that no human eye could see him. Behind every petal in the rose he had a bedroom. He was as well shaped and as handsome as any child could be, and had wings reaching from his shoulders right down to his feet. Oh! what a sweet smell there was in his room! And how bright and pretty were the walls of it! They were the pale pink, delicate rose leaves.

9 July

The Use of Colour

From *Wood and Garden, 1899* | Gertrude Jekyll (1843–1932)

I have always had great delight in the study of colour, as the word is understood by artists, which again is not a positive matter, but one of relation and proportion. And when one hears the common chatter about 'artistic colours' one receives an unpleasant impression about the education and good taste of the speaker; and one is reminded of an old saying which treats the unwisdom of rushing in 'where angels fear to tread,' and of regret that a good word should be degraded by misuse. It may be safely said that no colour can be called artistic in itself; for, in the first place it is bad English, and in the second, it is nonsense.

. . . .

They have no idea of using the colour of flowers as precious jewels in a setting of quiet environment, or of suiting the colour of flowering groups to that of the neighbouring foliage, thereby enhancing the value of both, or of massing related or harmonious colourings so as to lead up to the most powerful and brilliant effects; and yet all these are just the ways of employing colour to the best advantage.

Nymph of the Garden

From *Astrophil and Stella, written c.1581-1583* | Sir Philip Sidney
(1554–1586)

82.

Nymph of the garden where all beauties be;
   Beauties, which do in excellency pass
   His who till death looked in a watery glass,
Or hers whom naked the Trojan boy did see:
Sweet garden nymph, which keeps the cherry tree,
   Whose fruit doth far th'Hesperian taste surpass;
   Most sweet-fair, most fair-sweet, do not, alas,
From coming near those cherries banish me.
   For though, full of desire, empty of wit,
Admitted late by your best-graced grace,
I caught at one of them a hungry bit,
Pardon that fault, once more grant me the place,
And I do swear, even by the same delight,
   I will but kiss, I never more will bite.

The Vegetable or Kitchen Garden: Looking Ahead

From *The Beeton Book of Garden Management, 1862* | Samuel Orchart Beeton (1831–1877)

Probably this is the busiest month of the year in the kitchen garden, both on account of everything growing so fast, and because many crops have ceased to be useful, and must be removed and give place to others. We have to look forward to a long winter and spring, when vegetation is stationary or very slow; yet at that time it is necessary to have suitable crops; and now is the time to prepare the ground and get them in their places.

It is proper to observe that where rows of vegetables have previously grown, the ground is usually dry and hard. However moist the season has been, it will always be found different to that 18 inches or so on either side; it is not, therefore, advisable to crop immediately over the same spot; the difference will soon be observable between the rows planted exactly where peas have grown and those planted at the distance indicated. I have found it best not to plant winter crops on ground that has been newly-dug or trenched, and never knew broccoli do so well as when planted on hard ground that had not been dug since February; but when the plants had taken hold, and began to grow, the ground was forked over, and a dressing of manure worked in.

Refreshment

From *Villette, 1853* | Charlotte Brontë (1816–1855)

The orange-trees, and several plants, full and bright with bloom, basked also in the sun's laughing bounty; they had partaken it the whole day, and now asked water. M. Emanuel had a taste for gardening; he liked to tend and foster plants. I used to think that working amongst shrubs with a spade or a watering-pot soothed his nerves; it was a recreation to which he often had recourse; and now he looked to the orange-trees, the geraniums, the gorgeous cactuses, and revived them all with the refreshment their drought needed. His lips meantime sustained his precious cigar, that (for him) first necessary and prime luxury of life; its blue wreaths curled prettily enough amongst the flowers, and in the evening light.

13 July

A Farewell

Composed just before my sister and I went to fetch Mrs
Wordsworth from Gallow-hill, near Scarborough, 1802

William Wordsworth (1770–1850)

VERSES 1-4

Farewell, thou little Nook of mountain-ground,
Thou rocky corner in the lowest stair
Of that magnificent temple which doth bound
One side of our whole vale with grandeur rare;
Sweet garden-orchard, eminently fair,
The loveliest spot that man hath ever found,
Farewell! – we leave thee to Heaven's peaceful care,
Thee, and the Cottage which thou dost surround.

Our boat is safely anchored by the shore,
And there will safely ride when we are gone;
The flowering shrubs that deck our humble door
Will prosper, though untended and alone:
Fields, goods, and far-off chattels we have none:
These narrow bounds contain our private store
Of things earth makes, and sun doth shine upon;
Here are they in our sight – we have no more.

Sunshine and shower be with you, bud and bell!
For two months now in vain we shall be sought:
We leave you here in solitude to dwell
With these our latest gifts of tender thought;
Thou, like the morning, in thy saffron coat,
Bright gowan, and marsh-marigold, farewell!
Whom from the borders of the Lake we brought,
And placed together near our rocky Well.

We go for One to whom ye will be dear;
And she will prize this Bower, this Indian shed,
Our own contrivance, Building without peer!
- A gentle Maid, whose heart is lowly bred,
Whose pleasures are in wild fields gatherèd,
With joyousness, and with a thoughtful cheer,
Will come to you; to you herself will wed;
And love the blessed life that we lead here.

Mowing

From *The Wild Garden, 1870* | William Robinson (1838–1935)

Mowing the grass once a fortnight in pleasure grounds, as now practised, is a great and costly mistake. We want shaven carpets of grass here and there, but what cruel nonsense both to men and grass it is to shave as many foolish men shave their faces! There are indeed places where they boast of mowing forty acres! Who would not rather see the waving grass with countless flowers than a close shaven surface without a blossom? Imagine the labour wasted in this ridiculous labour of cutting the heads off flowers and grass. Let the grass grow till fit to cut for hay, and we may enjoy in it a world of lovely flowers that will blossom and perfect their growth before the grass has to be mown; more than one person who has carried out the ideas expressed in this book has waving lawns of feathery grass where he used to shave the grass every ten days; a prairie of flowers where a daisy was not allowed to peep; and some addition to his hay crop as he allows the grass to grow till it is fit for that purpose.

15 July

Happiness

From *My Ántonia, 1918* | Willa Cather (1873–1947)

JIM SITS IN THE GARDEN:

I sat down in the middle of the garden, where snakes could scarcely approach unseen, and leaned my back against a warm yellow pumpkin. There were some ground-cherry bushes growing along the furrows, full of fruit. I turned back the papery triangular sheaths that protected the berries and ate a few. All about me giant grasshoppers, twice as big as any I had ever seen, were doing acrobatic feats among the dried vines. The gophers scurried up and down the ploughed ground. There in the sheltered draw-bottom the wind did not blow very hard, but I could hear it singing its humming tune up on the level, and I could see the tall grasses wave. The earth was warm under me, and warm as I crumbled it through my fingers. Queer little red bugs came out and moved in slow squadrons around me. Their backs were polished vermilion, with black spots. I kept as still as I could. Nothing happened. I did not expect anything to happen. I was something that lay under the sun and felt it, like the pumpkins, and I did not want to be anything more. I was entirely happy. Perhaps we feel like that when we die and become a part of something entire, whether it is sun and air, or goodness and knowledge. At any rate, that is happiness; to be dissolved into something complete and great. When it comes to one, it comes as naturally as sleep.

Colour in the Flower Bed

From *Kew Gardens, 1919* | Virginia Woolf (1882–1941)

From the oval-shaped flower-bed there rose perhaps a hundred stalks spreading into heart-shaped or tongue-shaped leaves half way up and unfurling at the tip red or blue or yellow petals marked with spots of colour raised upon the surface; and from the red, blue or yellow gloom of the throat emerged a straight bar, rough with gold dust and slightly clubbed at the end.

The petals were voluminous enough to be stirred by the summer breeze, and when they moved, the red, blue and yellow lights passed one over the other, staining an inch of the brown earth beneath with a spot of the most intricate colour. The light fell either upon the smooth, grey back of a pebble, or the shell of a snail with its brown, circular veins, or falling into a raindrop, it expanded with such intensity of red, blue and yellow the thin walls of water that one expected them to burst and disappear. Instead, the drop was left in a second silver grey once more, and the light now settled upon the flesh of a leaf, revealing the branching thread of fibre beneath the surface, and again it moved on and spread its illumination in the vast green spaces beneath the dome of the heart-shaped and tongue-shaped leaves.

Then the breeze stirred rather more briskly overhead and the colour was flashed into the air above, into the eyes of the men and women who walk in Kew Gardens in July.

A Lincolnshire Lady's Grotto

From *Life of Johnson, 1791* | James Boswell (1740–1795)

'Would it not be a pretty cool habitation in summer, Mr Johnson?' she said.

'I think it would, Madam,' replied he, '– for a toad.'

The Scent of Lavender

From *The Garden Party, 1922* | Katherine Mansfield (1888–1923)

WORKMEN COME TO PUT UP THE MARQUEE:

Only the tall fellow was left. He bent down, pinched a sprig of lavender, put his thumb and forefinger to his nose and snuffed up the smell. When Laura saw that gesture she forgot all about the karakas in her wonder at him caring for things like that – caring for the smell of lavender. How many men that she knew would have done such a thing? Oh, how extraordinarily nice workmen were, she thought.

Lathyrus

From *The English Flower Garden, 1883* | William Robinson
(1838–1935)

Everlasting Pea: The perennial kinds of Peas are valuable, as they are of such free growth and last long in bloom. The kinds worth growing are not numerous, yet sufficient to keep up an unbroken display from May till October. Near a low wall or trellis they succeed admirably, and climbing gracefully drape such surfaces with veils of foliage and blossom. Upon banks, raised borders, or on the bold rock garden few things are prettier, and they never look better than when scrambling over the face of a rock, flowering as they go. The way to spoil them is to attempt to tie and train them in a stiff or formal way. They may be used with good effect in mixed borders, and they are valuable for cutting from. The best varieties are pretty if allowed to grow through beds of medium-sized shrubs, and there are few effects in gardens prettier than that of the best white varieties when allowed to trail and bloom on a grassy place untrained in any way; a few tufts so placed are charming and live for many years.

Come into the Garden

From *Maud, 1855* | Alfred, Lord Tennyson (1809–1892)

Part XXII, verses 1–3

Come into the garden, Maud,
　For the black bat, night, has flown,
Come into the garden, Maud,
　I am here at the gate alone;
And the woodbine spices are wafted abroad,
　And the musk of the rose is blown.

For a breeze of morning moves,
　And the planet of Love is on high,
Beginning to faint in the light that she loves
　In a bed of daffodil sky,
To faint in the light of the sun she loves,
　To faint in his light, and to die.

All night have the roses heard
　The flute, violin, bassoon;
All night has the casement jessamine stirr'd
　To the dancers dancing in tune;
Till a silence fell with the waking bird,
　And a hush with the setting moon.

The Prettiest Corner of the World

From *English Hours, 1870s, 1905* | Henry James (1843–1916)

English Vignettes V: Cambridge

If I were called upon, however, to mention the prettiest corner of the world, I should draw out a thoughtful sigh and point the way to the garden of Trinity Hall. My companion, who was very competent to judge (but who spoke indeed with the partiality of a son of the house), declared, as he ushered me into it, that it was, to his mind, the most beautiful small garden in Europe. I freely accepted, and I promptly repeat, an affirmation so magnanimously conditioned. The little garden at Trinity Hall is narrow and crooked; it leans upon the river, from which a low parapet, all muffled in ivy, divides it; it has an ancient wall adorned with a thousand matted creepers on one side, and on the other a group of extraordinary horse-chestnuts. The trees are of prodigious size; they occupy half the garden, and are remarkable for the fact that their giant limbs strike down into the earth, take root again and emulate, as they rise, the majesty of the parent stem. The manner in which this magnificent group of horse-chestnuts sprawls about over the grass, out into the middle of the lawn, is one of the most heart-shaking features of the garden of Trinity Hall.

Magic

From *The Secret Garden*, 1911 | Frances Hodgson Burnett (1849–1924)

'It's Magic,' said Mary, 'but not black. It's as white as snow.'

They always called it Magic and indeed it seemed like it in the
months that followed — the wonderful months — the radiant
months — the amazing ones. Oh! the things which happened
in that garden! If you have never had a garden you cannot
understand, and if you have had a garden you will know that it
would take a whole book to describe all that came to pass there.
At first it seemed that green things would never cease pushing
their way through the earth, in the grass, in the beds, even in the
crevices of the walls. Then the green things began to show buds
and the buds began to unfurl and show colour, every shade of
blue, every shade of purple, every tint and hue of crimson. In its
happy days flowers had been tucked away into every inch and hole
and corner. Ben Weatherstaff had seen it done and had himself
scraped out mortar from between the bricks of the wall and made
pockets of earth for lovely clinging things to grow on. Iris and
white lilies rose out of the grass in sheaves, and the green alcoves
filled themselves with amazing armies of the blue and white flower
lances of tall delphiniums or columbines or campanulas.

The View from a Prison Cell

From *The Kingis Quair, c.1423* | King James I of Scotland (1394–1437)

VERSES 30–32

30
Bewailing in my chamber thus alone,
  Despairing of all joy and remedy,
A-weary of my thoughts, and woe-begone,
  Unto the window did I walk in hye,
  To see the world and people walking by,
As at the time, though I of cheering food amusement
Might have nought else, to look it did me good

31
Now there was made fast by the tower wall
  A garden fair, and in the corners set
A herbere green, with wands so long and small
  Railed all about; and so with trees close set
  Was all the place, and hawthorn hedges knit.
That no one though he were near walking by,
Might there within scarce any one espy.

32
So thick the branches and the leafage green
  Beshaded all the alleys that there were.
And midst of ev'ry herbere might be seen
  The sharp and green sweet scented juniper,
  Growing so fair with branches here and there.
That, as it seemed to any one without.
The branches spread the herbere all about.

Proportion and Beauty in Plants

From *A Philosophical Enquiry into the Sublime and Beautiful*, 1757 | Edmund Burke (1729–1797)

Turning our eyes to the vegetable creation, we find nothing there so beautiful as flowers; but flowers are almost of every sort of shape, and of every sort of disposition; they are turned and fashioned into an infinite variety of forms; and from these forms botanists have given them their names, which are almost as various. What proportion do we discover between the stalks and the leaves of flowers, or between the leaves and the pistils? How does the slender stalk of the rose agree with the bulky head under which it bends? but the rose is a beautiful flower; and can we undertake to say that it does not owe a great deal of its beauty even to that disproportion; the rose is a large flower, yet it grows upon a small shrub; the flower of the apple is very small, and grows upon a large tree; yet the rose and the apple blossom are both beautiful, and the plants that bear them are most engagingly attired notwithstanding this disproportion. What by general consent is allowed to be a more beautiful object than an orange-tree, nourishing at once with its leaves, its blossoms, and its fruit? but it is in vain that we search here for any proportion between the height, the breadth, or anything else concerning the dimensions of the whole, or concerning the relation of the particular parts to each other.

25 July

To be done in the Parterre and Flower Garden: Box and Gravel-walks

From *Kalendarium Hortense, 1664* | John Evelyn (1620–1706)

Clip *Box*, &c. in *Parterres*, *Knots*, and *Compartiments*, if need be, and that it grow out of order: do it after *Rain*.

Take up your early *autumnal Cyclamen*, *Tulips*, and *Bulbs* (if you will *remove* them, &c.) before mentioned; *Transplanting* them *immediately*, or a *Month* after, if you please, and then cutting off and trimming the *Fibres*, spread them to air in some *dry* place. But separate not the *Off-sets* of *Tulips*, &c. until the *Mother Bulb* be fully dry.

Gather *Tulip-seed*, if you please; but let it lie in the *Pods*.

Now (in the *driest Season*) with *Lime*, *Brine*, *Pot-ashes* (which is the very best of all, because being cast on fine *Turf* it destroys the *Worms*, and improves the *Grass*, which most other Applications mortify), and *Water*, or a *Decoction* of *Tobacco Refuse*, water your *Gravel-walks*, &c. to destroy both *Worms* and *Weeds*, of which it will *cure* them for some *Years*.

A Lost Class of Men

From *Sketches by Boz, 1833–1836* | Charles Dickens (1812–1870)

There is another and a very different class of men, whose recreation is their garden. An individual of this class, resides some short distance from town – say in the Hampstead Road, or the Kilburn Road, or any other road where the houses are small and neat, and have little slips of back garden. He and his wife – who is as clean and compact a little body as himself – have occupied the same house ever since he retired from business twenty years ago. They have no family. They once had a son, who died at about five years old. The child's portrait hangs over the mantelpiece in the best sitting-room, and a little cart he used to draw about, is carefully preserved as a relic.

In fine weather the old gentleman is almost constantly in the garden; and when it is too wet to go into it, he will look out of the window at it, by the hour together. He has always something to do there, and you will see him digging, and sweeping, and cutting, and planting, with manifest delight. In spring-time, there is no end to the sowing of seeds, and sticking little bits of wood over them, with labels, which look like epitaphs to their memory; and in the evening, when the sun has gone down, the perseverance with which he lugs a great watering-pot about is perfectly astonishing. The only other recreation he has, is the newspaper, which he peruses every day, from beginning to end, generally reading the most interesting pieces of intelligence to his wife, during breakfast. The old lady is very fond of flowers, as the hyacinth-glasses in the parlour-window, and geranium-pots in the little front court, testify. She takes great pride in the garden too: and when one of the four fruit-trees produces rather a larger gooseberry than usual, it is carefully preserved under a wine-glass on the sideboard, for the edification of visitors, who are duly informed that Mr So-and-so planted the tree which produced it, with his own hands. On a summer's evening, when the large watering-pot has been filled and emptied some fourteen times, and the old couple have quite exhausted themselves by trotting about, you will see them sitting happily together in the little summerhouse, enjoying the calm and peace of the twilight, and watching the shadows as they fall upon the garden, and gradually growing thicker and more sombre, obscure the tints of their gayest flowers — no bad emblem of the years that have silently rolled over their heads, deadening in their course the brightest hues of early hopes and feelings which have long since faded away. These are their only recreations, and they require no more. They have within themselves, the materials of comfort and content; and the only anxiety of each, is to die before the other.

This is no ideal sketch. There used to be many old people of this description; their numbers may have diminished, and may decrease still more.

Ancient Roses

From *The Scented Garden, 1931* | Eleanour Sinclair Rohde (1881–1950)

We have not only caught and tamed the rose and changed
her character, but like the human race she differs through the
centuries. The roses depicted in the old missals and books of
hours in the pictures by the great masters and the stained glass
windows in our cathedrals resemble the roses of to-day as little
as the mediaeval mystic's outlook on life resembles that of the
modern scientist.

Archangel

From *Complete Herbal & English Physician, 1653* | Nicholas Culpeper (1616–1654)

LAMIUM:

Name: To put a gloss upon their practice, the physicians call an herb (which country people vulgarly know by the name of Dead Nettle) Archangel; whether they favour more of superstition or folly, I leave to the judicious reader.

. . . .

Place: They grow almost every way (unless it be in the middle of the street), the yellow most usually in the wet grounds of woods, and sometimes in the dryer, in divers counties of this nation.

. . . .

Government and virtues: It makes the heart merry, drives away melancholy, quickens the spirits, is good against quartan agues, stancheth bleeding at mouth and nose, if it be stamped and applied to the nape of the neck; the herb also bruised, and with some salt and vinegar and hog's-grease, laid upon a hard tumour or swelling, or that vulgarly called the king's evil, do help to dissolve or discuss them; and being in like manner applied, doth much allay the pains, and give ease to the gout, sciatica, and other pains of the joints and sinews. It is also very effectual to heal green wounds, and old ulcers; also to stay their fretting, gnawing, and spreading. It draws forth splinters, and such like things gotten into the flesh, and is very good against bruises and burnings.

The White House

From *Janet's Repentance, Scenes of Clerical Life*, 1857 | George
Eliot (1819–1880)

The garden was one of those old-fashioned paradises which
hardly exist any longer except as memories of our childhood: no
finical separation between flower and kitchen garden there; no
monotony of enjoyment for one sense to the exclusion of another;
but a charming paradisiacal mingling of all that was pleasant
to the eyes and good for food. The rich flower-border running
along every walk, with its endless succession of spring flowers,
anemones, auriculas, wall-flowers, sweet-williams, campanulas,
snapdragons, and tiger-lilies, had its taller beauties, such as
moss and Provence roses, varied with espalier apple-trees; the
crimson of a carnation was carried out in the lurking crimson
of the neighbouring strawberry-beds; you gathered a moss-rose
one moment and a bunch of currants the next; you were in a
delicious fluctuation between the scent of jasmine and the juice
of gooseberries. Then what a high wall at one end, flanked by a
summer-house so lofty, that after ascending its long flight of steps
you could see perfectly well there was no view worth looking at;
what alcoves and garden-seats in all directions; and along one side,
what a hedge, tall, and firm, and unbroken, like a green wall!

30 July

Bedding

From *My Garden in Summer, 1914* | E. A. Bowles (1865–1954)

I remember a garden of twenty years ago that was the most bedded I ever saw. Thousands of bedding plants were prepared for planting in Summer, but always in straight lines in long, straight borders. It began at the stable gates, and ran round three sides of the house, and continued in unbroken sequence, like Macbeth's vision of kings, for two sides of a croquet lawn, and then rushed up one side and down the other of a long path starting at right angles from the middle of the lawn, and if you began at the gates with Blue Lobelia, Mrs Pollock Pelargonium, Perilla, Yellow Calceolaria, and some Scarlet Pelargonium in ranks according to their relative stature, so you continued for yards, poles, perches, furlongs, or whatever it was – I hate measures, and purposely forget them – and so you ended up when the border brought you back again to the lawn. I once suggested, Why not paint the ground in stripes, and have the effect all year round, even if snow had to be swept off sometimes? I know an instance of a stately, formal garden which was so expensive to fill with gay flowers that its owner had coloured tiles made to lay in the beds.

AUGUST

The Air Stirred with Scent

Objection No. 1

From *Observations on the Theory and Practice of Landscape Gardening, 1803* | Humphrey Repton (1752–1818)

There is no error more prevalent in modern gardening, or more frequently carried to excess, than taking away hedges to unite many small fields into one extensive and naked lawn, before plantations are made to give it the appearance of a park; and where ground is subdivided by sunk fences, imaginary freedom is dearly purchased at the expense of actual confinement.
[The first of ten objections]

Retreat

From *In Memoriam, 1850* | Alfred, Lord Tennyson (1809–1892)

PART LXXXIX, VERSES 1–4

Witch-elms that counterchange the floor
   Of this flat lawn with dusk and bright,
   And thou, with all thy breadth and height
Of foliage, towering sycamore;

How often, hither wandering down,
   My Arthur found your shadows fair,
   And shook to all the liberal air
The dust and din and steam of town:

He brought an eye for all he saw;
   He mixt in all our simple sports;
   They pleased him, fresh from brawling courts
And dusty purlieus of the law.

O joy to him in this retreat,
   Immantled in ambrosial dark,
   To drink the cooler air, and mark
The landscape winking thro' the heat.

Lingering Dews

From *Under the Greenwood Tree, 1872* | Thomas Hardy (1840–1928)

It was a morning of the latter summer-time; a morning of
lingering dews, when the grass is never dry in the shade.
Fuchsias and dahlias were laden till eleven o'clock with small
drops and dashes of water, changing the colour of their sparkle at
every movement of the air; and elsewhere hanging on twigs like
small silver fruit. The threads of garden-spiders appeared thick
and polished. In the dry and sunny places, dozens of long-legged
crane-flies whizzed off the grass at every step the passer took.

3 August

Dragons

From *Complete Herbal & English Physician, 1653* | Nicholas
Culpeper (1616–1654)

DRACONTIUM:

They are so well known to all those who plant them in their
gardens, they need no description; if not, let them look down to
the lower end of the stalks, and see how like a snake they look.

Government and virtues: The plant is under the dominion of
Mars, and therefore it would be a wonder if it should want some
obnoxious quality or other: In all herbs of that quality, the safest
way is either to distil the herb in an alembick, in what vehicle
you please, or else to press out the juice, and distil that in a glass
still, in sand. It scours and cleanses the internal parts of the body
mightily, and it clears the external parts also, being externally
applied, from freckles, morphew, and sun-burning: Your best
way to use it externally, is to mix it with vinegar; an ointment of
it is held to be good in wounds and ulcers; it consumes cankers,
and that flesh growing in the nostrils, which they call polypus:
Also the distilled water being dropped into the eyes, takes away
spots there, or the pin and web, and mends the dimness of sight;
it is excellently good against pestilence and poison. Pliny and
Dioscorides affirm, that no serpent will meddle with him that
carries this herb about him.

The Starting Point

From *Cotswolds Gardens, 1995* | David Hicks (1929–1998)

My own interest in gardening started when I was eight years
old. It was at this point that my parents gave me a small plot,
four feet square, in their own garden. Here I was given my head
and allowed to grow a haphazard collection of garishly coloured
annuals. Later I was to spend hours driving my mother, and the
local nursery owner, to the point of distraction with unending
questions about this type of shrub and that type of herbaceous
perennial. I designed my first complete garden when I was 15.
This was when we moved to Suffolk, and it was there that I
first experimented with scale, which I believe is the single most
important factor in creating a successful garden.

5 August

The Vegetable or Kitchen Garden: Tomatoes and Spinach

From *The Beeton Book of Garden Management, 1862* | Samuel Orchart Beeton (1831–1877)

Tomatoes — These should be carefully trained, and stopped as they grow. Stop just over a bunch of flowers, and leave no more shoots than can be conveniently trained. Unless the ground is very dry, they do not require watering, and will most probably do best without it.

Spinach — About the second week in this month sow the main crop of winter spinach: where a good supply of this is wanted, it would be best to sow every week this month. The earliest sown will grow quickly, but the later will stand the winter best, and prove valuable in the spring: sow in drills a foot apart, or sow, thinly, broadcast, treading it in either case.

A Golden Deed

From *The Wouldbegoods, 1901* | E. Nesbit (1858–1924)

We agreed to get up the very next day, ere yet the rosy dawn had flushed the east, and have a go at Mrs Simpkins's garden:
We looked at the garden. It was very neat. Only one patch was coming up thick with weeds. I could see groundsel and chickweed, and others that I did not know. We set to work with a will. We used all our tools – spades, forks, hoes, and rakes – and Dora worked with the trowel, sitting down, because her foot was hurt. We cleared the weedy patch beautifully, scraping off all the nasty weeds and leaving the nice clean brown dirt. We worked as hard as ever we could. And we were happy, because it was unselfish toil, and no one thought then of putting it in the Book of Golden Deeds, where we had agreed to write down our virtuous actions and the good doings of each other, when we happen to notice them.

We had just done, and we were looking at the beautiful production of our honest labour, when the cottage door burst open, and the soldier's widowed mother came out like a wild tornado, and her eyes looked like upas trees – death to the beholder.

'You wicked, meddlesome, nasty children!' she said, 'ain't you got enough of your own good ground to runch up and spoil but you must come into my little lot?'

Some of us were deeply alarmed, but we stood firm.

'We have only been weeding your garden,' Dora said; 'we wanted to do something to help you.'

'Dratted little busybodies,' she said. It was indeed hard, but everyone in Kent says 'dratted' when they are cross. 'It's my turnips,' she went on, 'you've hoed up, and my cabbages. My turnips that my boy sowed afore he went. There, get along with you, do, afore I come at you with my broom-handle.'

She did come at us with her broom-handle as she spoke, and even the boldest turned and fled.

Oswald was even the boldest.

'They looked like weeds right enough,' he said.

And Dicky said, 'It all comes of trying to do golden deeds.'

The Parks and Gardens of Scotland

From *The Expedition of Humphry Clinker, vol III, 1771* | Tobias Smollett (1721–1771)

EDINBURGH, AUGUST 8

To Dr Lewis

I should be very ungrateful, dear Lewis, if I did not find myself disposed to think and speak favourably of this people, among whom I have met with more kindness, hospitality, and rational entertainment, in a few weeks, than ever I received in any other country during the whole course of my life.

. . . .

Though the villas of the Scotch nobility and gentry have generally an air of grandeur and state, I think their gardens and parks are not comparable to those of England; a circumstance the more remarkable, as I was told by the ingenious Mr Phillip Miller of Chelsea, that almost all the gardeners of South-Britain were natives of Scotland. The verdure of this country is not equal to that of England. – The pleasure-grounds are, in my opinion, not so well laid out according to the genus loci; nor are the lawns, and walks, and hedges kept in such delicate order. – The trees are planted in prudish rows, which have not such an agreeable natural effect, as when they are thrown into irregular groupes, with intervening glades; and the firs, which they generally raise around their houses, look dull and funereal in the summer season. – I must confess, indeed, that they yield serviceable timber, and good shelter against the northern blasts; that they grow and thrive in the most barren soil, and continually perspire a fine balsam of turpentine, which must render the air very salutary and sanative to lungs of a tender texture.

. . . .

Yours always,
Matt. Bramble

Labours

From *Rural Rides, 1830* | William Cobbett (1763–1835)

St Albans

It is curious to observe how the different labours are divided as to the nations. The mowers are all English; the haymakers all Irish. Scotchmen toil hard enough in Scotland, but when they go from home it is not to work, if you please. They are found in gardens, and especially in gentlemen's gardens. Tying up flowers, picking dead leaves off exotics, peeping into melon-frames, publishing the banns of marriage between the 'male' and 'female' blossoms, tap-tap-tapping against a wall with a hammer that weighs half an ounce. They have backs as straight and shoulders as square as heroes of Waterloo; and who can blame them? The digging, the mowing, the carrying of loads, all the break back and sweat extracting work, they leave to be performed by those who have less prudence than they have.

9 August

The Best Sport in the World

From *We Made a Garden, 1956* | Margery Fish (1892–1969)

THE BANK ROUND THE ORCHARD NEEDED CLEARING:

Walter and the garden boy had other big jobs on hand, and it was considered too much of an undertaking for me.

But in the end I got it done. One of my sisters providentially came for a holiday and helped me clear the weeds from the bank. We had a magnificent time clearing the ground, because there was a lot of bindweed there, as well as the easier weeds. We both agreed that there is no sport in the world that compares with clearing ground of bindweed. It is far more exciting than golf or fishing. Tracing this tenacious creeping Judas of a weed to its source and getting it out without leaving any small broken pieces behind requires skill and patience, and the reward is a barrowload of the obscene twisting white roots and the joy of burning them.

10 August

A Sundial from the Old Country

From *Emily of New Moon, 1923* | L. M. Montgomery (1874–1942)

The garden was a beautiful place, well worthy Cousin Jimmy's
pride. It seemed like a garden where no frost could wither or
rough wind blow – a garden remembering a hundred vanished
summers. There was a high hedge of clipped spruce all around it,
spaced at intervals by tall lombardies. The north side was closed
in by a thick grove of spruce against which a long row of peonies
grew, their great red blossoms splendid against its darkness. One
big spruce grew in the centre of the garden and underneath it
was a stone bench, made of flat shore stones worn smooth by
long polish of wind and wave. In the south-east corner was an
enormous clump of lilacs, trimmed into the semblance of one
large drooping-boughed tree, gloried over with purple. An old
summer house, covered with vines, filled the south-west corner.
And in the north-west corner there was a sundial of grey stone,
placed just where the broad red walk that was bordered with
striped grass, and picked out with pink conchs, ran off into Lofty
John's bush. Emily had never seen a sundial before and hung over
it enraptured.

'Your great-great-grandfather, Hugh Murray, had that brought
from the Old Country,' said Cousin Jimmy. 'There isn't as fine a
one in the Maritime Provinces.'

Wasps

From *The Natural History and Antiquities of Selborne, 1789*

Gilbert White (1720–1793)

Letter LXIV to The Honourable Daines Barrington

The great pests of a garden are wasps, which destroy all the finer fruits just as they are coming into perfection. In 1781 we had none; in 1783 there were myriads; which would have devoured all the produce of my garden, had not we set the boys to take the nests, and caught thousands with hazel twigs tipped with bird-lime: we have since employed the boys to take and destroy the large breeding wasps in the spring. Such expedients have a great effect on these marauders, and will keep them under. Though wasps do not abound but in hot summers, yet they do not prevail in every hot summer, as I have instanced in the two years above-mentioned.

Jewels in Moonlight

From *Sybil, 1845* | Benjamin Disraeli (1804–1881)

The moonbeam fell upon the roof and garden of Gerard. It
suffused the cottage with its brilliant light, except where the
dark depth of the embowered porch defied its entry. All around
the beds of flowers and herbs spread sparkling and defined. You
could trace the minutest walk; almost distinguish every leaf. Now
and then there came a breath, and the sweet-peas murmured in
their sleep; or the roses rustled, as if they were afraid they were
about to be roused from their lightsome dreams. Farther on the
fruit-trees caught the splendour of the night; and looked like a
troop of sultanas taking their gardened air, when the eye of man
could not profane them, and laden with jewels. There were apples
that rivalled rubies; pears of topaz tint: a whole paraphernalia
of plums, some purple as the amethyst, others blue and brilliant
as the sapphire; an emerald here, and now a golden drop that
gleamed like the yellow diamond of Gengis Khan.

August

From *My Garden in Summer, 1914* | E. A. Bowles (1865–1954)

August is always supposed to be a bad month for gardens, a breathing-space for the flowers between the rush of summer Roses and the best herbaceous plants and the final flare-up of Asters and Sunflowers and Dahlias and the other gorgeous things of early Autumn; so I have made a practice when in gardens or nurseries of noting plants that are good in August and trying them here, therefore my garden has something good to show throughout the month, unless the Clerk of the Weather refuses us any rain.

14 August

The Garden that I Love

From *The Gardener's Daughter, 1842* | Alfred, Lord Tennyson
(1809–1892)

Not wholly in the busy world, nor quite
Beyond it, blooms the garden that I love.
News from the humming city comes to it
In sound of funeral or of marriage bells;
And, sitting muffled in dark leaves, you hear
The windy clanging of the minster clock;
Although between it and the garden lies
A league of grass, wash'd by a slow broad stream,
That, stirr'd with languid pulses of the oar,
Waves all its lazy lilies, and creeps on,
Barge-laden, to three arches of a bridge
Crown'd with the minster-towers.

Kitchen Gardens

From *The Scots Gardener, 1683* | John Reid (1656–1723)

Of all gardens the kitchen-garden is the best. In every garden it
is ordinary, first, to make a border at the wall; secondly, a walk;
and, thirdly, a border on the other side of the walk: thus the
walk, with a border on each side of it, going round the whole
plot, parallel to the wall: but if your ground be large enough, I
would advise you to make a larger distance betwixt the walk and
the wall. It is also ordinary to divide the garden into four plots,
by two walks crossing from side to side: tho' I do not approve
of cross-walks in gardens yet if you would have more than one,
which divides the whole into two parts, make them all parallel
through the plot, leading to the house, and equi-distant from the
middle, still making the gates, doors, or entries, front the walks.

Evening Falls

From *The Man of Property, 1906* | John Galsworthy (1867–1933)

The little garden had fallen into shade, the sun now only reached
the wall at the end, whereon basked a crouching cat, her yellow
eyes turned sleepily down on the dog Balthasar. There was a
drowsy hum of very distant traffic; the creepered trellis round
the garden shut out everything but sky, and house, and pear-tree,
with its top branches still gilded by the sun.

Knots or Tarts

From *The Essays or Counsels, Civil and Moral: On Gardening, 1625* | Francis Bacon (1561–1626)

As for the making of knots or figures, with divers coloured earths, that they may lie under the windows of the house on that side which the garden stands, they be but toys: you may see as good sights, many times in tarts.

A Little Boy and a Little Girl

From *The Snow Queen, 1844* | Hans Christian Andersen (1805–1875) |
Translated by M. R. James (1862–1936)

In the big town, where there are so many houses and people that there isn't room enough for everybody to have a little garden, and where in consequence most people have to content themselves with flowers in pots, there were two poor children who had a garden somewhat bigger than a flower-pot. They weren't brother and sister, but they were as fond of each other as if they had been. Their parents were near neighbours, living in two attics, where the roof of the one house touched the other, and the gutter ran along the eaves: a small window in each house faced the other; you had only to step across the gutter and you could get from one window to the other.

The parents had, each of them, a large wooden box outside the window, and in it grew kitchen herbs which they used, and also a little rose tree; there was one in each box, and they flourished wonderfully. Then the parents thought of putting the boxes across the gutter in such a way that they reached almost from the one window to the other and really looked like two bunches of flowers. The pea plants hung down over the boxes, and the rose trees put out long branches and twined about the windows and bent over to meet each other, and made almost a triumphal arch of leaves and blossoms. The boxes were very high up, and the children knew they must not climb up into them, but they were often allowed to get out to meet each other and sit on their little stools beneath the roses, and there they used to play very happily.

First Plants

From *The Education of a Gardener, 1962* | Russell Page (1906–1985)

I started to understand something about plants by handling them. It was on one summer holiday when I was perhaps fourteen that, bored with the riding and jumping competitions at a local agricultural show, I wandered off to the flower-tent. There in an atmosphere hot and heavy with the smell of trampled grass, people, animals and flowers, my attention was caught by a tiny plant of *Campanula pulla* with three deep purple bells, huge in comparison with its frail leaves and the minute pot in which it grew. It was mine for a shilling and it opened a new world for me. I had no idea what to do for it or how to make it flourish in the cold clay of a Lincolnshire garden. So I went off to the public library and within a few days I had found friends and teachers in Reginald Farrer with his *English Rock Garden* and Gertrude Jekyll with *Wall and Water Garden,* two people who had spent a life time with plants and gardens.

All my pocket money went on rock plants. All my holidays were given to my own personal corner of the garden. I would bicycle for miles to get a basket of leaf-soil, I would steal grit, sand or gravel from roadside heaps and I would borrow a horse and cart to collect stones which were hard to come by in our stoneless countryside. My campanula died but meanwhile I had seen a picture of *Primula farinosa,* fallen in love with it and learned that it grew wild in Yorkshire. I had to lure my father, who liked bird-watching, into the Yorkshire dales. There I walked miles questioning every passer-by and after three weeks' search I eventually found an abandoned quarry starred with the pale mauve treasures that I sought.

Pruning and Weeding

From *Richard II, dated 1595–1596* | William Shakespeare (1564–1616)

ACT III, SCENE IV

Gardener

To *First Man:* Go, bind thou up yon dangling apricots
Which, like unruly children, make their sire
Stoop with oppression of their prodigal weight.
Give some supportance to the bending twigs.
To Second Man: Go thou, and, like an executioner,
Cut off the heads of too fast-growing sprays,
That look too lofty in our commonwealth:
All must be even in our government.
You thus employed, I will go root away
The noisome weeds, which without profit suck
The soil's fertility from wholesome flowers.

First Man

Why should we, in the compass of a pale,
Keep law and form and due proportion,
Showing, as in a model, our firm estate,
When our sea-wallèd garden, the whole land,
Is full of weeds, her fairest flowers choked up,
Her fruit-trees all unpruned, her hedges ruined,
Her knots disordered and her wholesome herbs
Swarming with caterpillars?

Gardener
Hold thy peace.
He that hath suffered this disordered spring
Hath now himself met with the fall of leaf.
The weeds which his broad-spreading leaves did shelter,
That seemed in eating him to hold him up,
Are plucked up root and all by Bolingbroke −
I mean the Earl of Wiltshire, Bushy, Green.

Second Man
What, are they dead?

Gardener
They are; and Bolingbroke
Hath seized the wasteful king. O, what pity is it
That he had not so trimmed and dressed his land
As we this garden! We at time of year
Do wound the bark, the skin of our fruit-trees,
Lest, being over-proud in sap and blood,
With too much riches it confound itself.
Had he done so to great and growing men,
They might have lived to bear, and he to taste
Their fruits of duty. Superfluous branches
We lop away, that bearing boughs may live.
Had he done so, himself had borne the crown,
Which waste of idle hours hath quite thrown down.

Useful Plants

From *Memories and Portraits, 1887* | Robert Louis Stevenson
(1850–1894)

An old Scotch gardener:
The very truth was that he scorned all flowers together. They
were but garnishings, childish toys, trifling ornaments for ladies'
chimney-shelves. It was towards his cauliflowers and peas and
cabbage that his heart grew warm. His preference for the more
useful growths was such that cabbages were found invading the
flower-pots, and an outpost of savoys was once discovered in the
centre of the lawn.

22 August

277

A Wall and a Mulberry Tree

From *The Awkward Age, 1898–1899* | Henry James (1843–1916)

Mr Longdon's garden took in three acres and, full of charming
features, had for its greatest wonder the extent and colour of
its old brick wall, in which the pink and purple surface was the
fruit of the mild ages and the protective function, for a visitor
strolling, sitting, talking, reading, that of a nurse of reverie. The
air of the place, in the August time, thrilled all the while with
the bliss of birds, the hum of little lives unseen and the flicker of
white butterflies.

. . . .

There were sitting-places, just there, out of the full light, cushioned
benches in the thick wide spread of old mulberry-boughs.

To be done in the Parterre and Flower Garden: Bartholomew-tide

From *Kalendarium Hortense, 1664* | John Evelyn (1620–1706)

Now (and not till *now*, if you expect *success*) is the just *Season* for the *budding* of the *Orange-Tree. Inoculate,* therefore, at the commencement of this *Month,* upon *seedling Stocks* of four Years growth. And to have excellent *Buds,* cut off the *Head* of some very old *Orange-tree* of a good kind, which making large *Shoots,* will furnish the best.

You may now sow *Narcissus* and *Oriental Jacinths,* and replant such as will not do well out of the *Earth;* as *Fritillaria, Hyacinths, Martagon, Dens Caninus, Lillies.*

Now, about *Bartholomew-tide,* is the only *secure Season* for *removing* and *laying* your *perennial Greens, Oranges, Lemons, Myrtles, Phillyreas, Oleanders, Jasmines, Arbutus,* and other rare *Shrubs,* as *Pomegranades, Monthly-Roses,* and whatever is most obnoxious to *Frosts;* taking the *Shoots* and *Branches* of the past *Spring,* and pegging them down in very *rich Earth,* and *Soil* perfectly consum'd, *watering* them upon all occasions during the *Summer;* and by this time *twelve-month* they will be ready to *remove, transplanted* in fit Earth, set in the *shade,* and kept moderately *moist,* not *over-*wet, lest the young *Fibres* rot; after *three* Weeks set them in some more airy place, but not in the *Sun* till fifteen days more.

Ah! Sun-Flower

From *Songs of Experience, 1789* | William Blake (1757–1827)

Ah, Sun-flower! weary of time,
Who countest the steps of the sun,
Seeking after that sweet golden clime
Where the traveller's journey is done.

Where the Youth pined away with desire,
And the pale Virgin shrouded in snow:
Arise from their graves, and aspire,
Where my Sun-flower wishes to go.

25 August

Watering

From *The Gardener's Year, 1929* | Karel Čapek (1890–1938) | Translated by Marie Weatherall (1897–1972) and Robert Weatherall (1899–1973)

One would think that watering a little garden is quite a simple thing, especially if one has a hose. It will soon be clear that until it has been tamed a hose is an extraordinarily evasive and dangerous beast, for it contorts itself, it jumps, it wriggles, it makes puddles of water, and dives with delight into the mess it has made; then it goes for the man who is going to use it and coils itself round his legs; you must hold it down with your foot, and then it rears and twists round your waist and neck, and while you are fighting with it as with a cobra, the monster turns up its brass mouth and projects a mighty stream of water through the windows on to the curtains which have been recently hung. You must grasp it firmly, and hold it tight; the beast rears with pain, and begins to spout water, not from the mouth, but from the hydrant and from somewhere in the middle of its body. Three men at least are needed to tame it at first, and they will all leave the place of battle splashed to the ears with mud and drenched with water; as to the garden itself, in parts it has changed into greasy pools, while in other places it is cracking with thirst.

Scent at Night

From *Sons and Lovers, 1913* | D. H. Lawrence (1885–1930)

The beauty of the night made him want to shout. A half moon, dusky gold, was sinking behind the black sycamore at the end of the garden, making the sky dull purple with its glow. Nearer, a dim white fence of lilies went across the garden, and the air all round seemed to stir with scent, as if it were alive. He went across the bed of pinks, whose keen perfume came sharply across the rocking, heavy scent of the lilies, and stood alongside the white barrier of flowers. They flagged all loose, as if they were panting. The scent made him drunk.

The Delight of an Orchard

From *A New Orchard and Garden, 1618* | William Lawson

(c.1554–1635)

What can your eye desire to see, your ears to heare, your mouth to taste, or your nose to smell, that is not to be had in an Orchard, with abundance and variety? What more delightsome than an infinite variety of sweet smelling flowers? decking with sundry coloures, the greene mantle of the Earth, the universall Mother of us all, so by them bespotted, so dyed, that all the world cannot sample them, and wherein it is more fit to admire the Dyer, than imitate his workmanship. Colouring not onely the earth, but decking the ayre, and sweetening every breath and spirit.

The Game of the Earthly Paradise

From *Mary's Meadow In Aunt Judy's Magazine, 1883–1884*

Juliana Horatia Ewing (1841–1885)

MARY'S IDEA:

'Wouldn't it be a good new game to have an Earthly Paradise
in our gardens, and to have a King's Apothecary and Herbalist
to gather things and make medicine of them, and an Honest
Rootgatherer to divide the polyanthus plants and bulbs when we
take them up, and divide them fairly, and a Weeding Woman
to work and make things tidy, and a Queen in a blue dress, and
Saxon [the dog] for the Dwarf.'

. . . .

MARY WANTS TO BE THE WEEDING WOMAN:

'I had no wish to be Queen, as far as that went. Dressing up, and
walking about the garden would be no fun for me. I really had
looked forward to clearing away big baskets of weeds and rubbish,
and keeping our five gardens and the paths between them so tidy
as they had never been kept before.'

Behind a Wall

Amy Lowell (1874–1925)

I own a solace shut within my heart,
   A garden full of many a quaint delight
   And warm with drowsy, poppied sunshine; bright,
Flaming with lilies out of whose cups dart
      Shining things
      With powdered wings.

Here terrace sinks to terrace, arbors close
   The ends of dreaming paths; a wanton wind
   Jostles the half-ripe pears, and then, unkind,
Tumbles a-slumber in a pillar rose,
      With content
      Grown indolent.

By night my garden is o'erhung with gems
   Fixed in an onyx setting. Fireflies
   Flicker their lanterns in my dazzled eyes.
In serried rows I guess the straight, stiff stems
      Of hollyhocks
      Against the rocks.

So far and still it is that, listening,
   I hear the flowers talking in the dawn;
   And where a sunken basin cuts the lawn,
Cinctured with iris, pale and glistening,
      The sudden swish
      Of a waking fish.

30 August

Green Brains

From *My Garden, 1971* | H. E. Bates (1905–1974)

We hear much of green fingers, but nothing of green brains. Clearly, however, it is possible sometimes to learn things that one is not born with. That this is true of gardening is well illustrated by a friend of mine who had never gardened in her entire life until suddenly inspired by a large new greenhouse her husband had bought himself. When she invited me to view the first results of her labours I was astonished to find an almost professional array of flowers, seedlings, boxes of annuals, tomatoes and so on. When I expressed astonishment, to which I added much congratulation, she made the sensible but disarming reply:

'Well I can read, can't I?'

SEPTEMBER

No Noise Except the Birds and Bees

Trespassers Will Be . . .

From *The Posthumous Papers of the Pickwick Club, 1837*

Charles Dickens (1812–1870)

AFTER AN EXCELLENT PICNIC LUNCH ON CAPTAIN BOLDWIG'S LAND, MR PICKWICK FALLS ASLEEP IN THE WHEELBARROW:

Captain Boldwig was a little fierce man in a stiff black neckerchief and blue surtout, who, when he did condescend to walk about his property, did it in company with a thick rattan stick with a brass ferrule, and a gardener and sub-gardener with meek faces, to whom (the gardeners, not the stick) Captain Boldwig gave his orders with all due grandeur and ferocity; for Captain Boldwig's wife's sister had married a marquis, and the captain's house was a villa, and his land 'grounds,' and it was all very high, and mighty, and great.

Mr Pickwick had not been asleep half an hour when little Captain Boldwig, followed by the two gardeners, came striding along as fast as his size and importance would let him; and when he came near the oak tree, Captain Boldwig paused and drew a long breath, and looked at the prospect as if he thought the prospect ought to be highly gratified at having him to take notice of it; and then he struck the ground emphatically with his stick, and summoned the head-gardener.

'Hunt,' said Captain Boldwig.

'Yes, sir,' said the gardener.

'Roll this place to-morrow morning – do you hear, Hunt?'

'Yes, sir.'

'And take care that you keep me this place in good order – do you hear, Hunt?'

'Yes, sir.'

'And remind me to have a board done about trespassers, and spring guns, and all that sort of thing, to keep the common people out. Do you hear, Hunt; do you hear?'

'I'll not forget it, sir.'

Colour and Time

From *The Morville Hours, 2008* | Katherine Swift (1956–)

Colour is seeping back into the garden. Leaves sparkle, washed of the dust of August. The grass is greening up again; the red of the dahlias vibrates against the glossy evergreens of the tapestry hedge. The angle of the sun is lower now, making the light redder and less intense, enhancing pure reds and their complementary greens.

I sit in the sun in the west-facing arbour of the Cloister Garden, one of the cats on my knees. The sun moves down the sky. I feel no inclination to read or work; I merely sit. It is paradoxical that, as the days grow shorter, I should feel this sudden expansion of time. Yesterday we finished clipping the yew hedges. There are stray fronds still scattered about the grass. Now, nearly twenty years after the garden began to be made, the hedges are seven feet tall, wrapping the garden round, lapping it with green in this bleached, post-harvest landscape.

The wound-up watch-spring of summer is winding down. The days fill with rounded golden light, like rich old Sauternes, full and sweet. Sugars caramelise in the leaves – tones of butterscotch, cinder toffee, treacle tart; quince paste, marmalade, toffee apple; Beaujolais, cassis, Lynch-Bages. The hedgerow shines with great plates and bunches of glossy berries like so many jars of jelly and jam ranged on a larder shelf – scarlet hip and crimson haw; red bullace and yellow crab; purple elderberry and blue-black sloe. Trees blaze, as if reverse photosynthesis were taking place, green chlorophyll turning back into pure energy.

The Life of a Plant Hunter in Canada

From *Journal, 1825* | David Douglas (1799–1834)

TRAVELLING UP THE SUMMIT ON THE NORTH SIDE OF THE GRAND
RAPIDS:

This took three days, and was one of the most laborious
undertakings I ever experienced, the way was so rough, over dead
wood, detached rocks, rivulets, &c. that very little paper could
be carried. Indeed I was obliged to leave my blanket (which, on
my route is all my bedding) at my first encampment about two-
thirds up. My provision was 3 oz. tea, 1 lb. sugar, and four small
biscuits. On the summit all the herbage is low shrub but chiefly
herb plants. The second day I caught no fish, and at such a great
altitude the only birds to be seen were hawks, eagles, vultures,
&c. I was fortunate enough to kill one young white-headed eagle,
which (then) I found very good eating. On the summit of the hill
I slept one night. I made a small fire of grass and twigs and dried
my clothes which were wet with perspiration and then laid myself
down on the grass with my feet in the fire. I found it very cold and
had to rise four times and walk to keep myself warm. Fortunately
it was dry and a keen north wind prevented dew.

3 September

For These

Edward Thomas (1878–1917)

An acre of land between the shore and the hills,
Upon a ledge that shows my kingdoms three,
The lovely visible earth and sky and sea
Where what the curlew needs not, the farmer tills:

A house that shall love me as I love it,
Well-hedged, and honoured by a few ash trees
That linnets, greenfinches, and goldfinches
Shall often visit and make love in and flit:

A garden I need never go beyond,
Broken but neat, whose sunflowers every one
Are fit to be the sign of the Rising Sun:
A spring, a brook's bend, or at least a pond:

For these I ask not, but, neither too late
Nor yet too early, for what men call content,
And also that something may be sent
To be contented with, I ask of Fate.

A Garden in the Country

From *The Tale of Johnny Town-Mouse, 1918* | Beatrix Potter
(1866–1943)

Timmy Willie longed to be at home in his peaceful nest in a
sunny bank. The food disagreed with him; the noise prevented
him from sleeping. In a few days he grew so thin that Johnny
Town-mouse noticed it, and questioned him. He listened to
Timmy Willie's story and inquired about the garden. 'It sounds
rather a dull place? What do you do when it rains?'

'When it rains, I sit in my little sandy burrow and shell corn
and seeds from my Autumn store. I peep out at the throstles and
blackbirds on the lawn, and my friend Cock Robin. And when
the sun comes out again, you should see my garden and the
flowers – roses and pinks and pansies – no noise except the birds
and bees, and the lambs in the meadows.'

Gossamer Webs

From *Kilvert's Diary, 1875* | Francis Kilvert (1840–1879)

6 September

All night the heavy drenching fog brooded over the land,
clinging to the meadows long after the sun was risen, and it was
not until after he had gained some height in the sky that he was
able to break through and dispel the mists. Then the morning
suddenly became glorious and we saw what had happened in
the night. All night long millions of gossamer spiders had been
spinning and the whole country was covered as if with one vast
fairy web. They spread over lawn and meadow grass and gate
and hawthorn hedge, and as the morning sun glinted upon their
delicate threads drenched and beaded with the film of the mist
the gossamer webs gleamed and twinkled into crimson and gold
and green, like the most exquisite shot-silk dress in the finest
texture of gauzy silver wire. I never saw anything like it or
anything so exquisite as 'the Virgin's webs' glowed with changing
opal lights and glanced with all the colours of the rainbow.

Travelling to the Future

From *News from Nowhere, 1890* | William Morris (1834–1896)

WILLIAM GUEST TRAVELS FORWARD IN TIME TO A DIFFERENT
ENGLAND:

And now again I was busy looking about me, for we were quite
clear of Piccadilly Market, and were in a region of elegantly
built, much ornamented houses, which I should have called villas
if they had been ugly and pretentious, which was very far from
being the case. Each house stood in a garden carefully cultivated,
and running over with flowers. The blackbirds were singing their
best amid the garden-trees, which, except for a bay here and
there, and occasional groups of limes, seemed to be all fruit-
trees. There were a great many cherry-trees, now all laden with
fruit; and several times as we passed by a garden we were offered
baskets of fine fruit by children and young girls. Amid all these
gardens and houses it was of course impossible to trace the sites of
the old streets; but it seemed to me that the main roadways were
the same as of old.

7 September

The Vegetable or Kitchen Garden: Winter Vegetables

From *The Beeton Book of Garden Management, 1862* | Samuel Orchart Beeton (1831–1877)

To secure a supply of vegetables in the winter and early spring, all arrangements not already completed should now be made without delay; the growth of those already planted encouraged by hoeing and stirring the earth round the roots, and where slugs abound, their ravages counteracted by sowing soot or lime on the soil.

The Garden in September

Lines 1-18 | Robert Bridges (1844–1930)

Now thin mists temper the slow-ripening beams
Of the September sun: his golden gleams
On gaudy flowers shine, that prank the rows
Of high-grown hollyhocks, and all tall shows
That Autumn flaunteth in his bushy bowers;
Where tomtits, hanging from the drooping heads
Of giant sunflowers, peck the nutty seeds;
And in the feathery aster bees on wing
Seize and set free the honied flowers,
Till thousand stars leap with their visiting:
While ever across the path mazily flit,
Unpiloted in the sun,
The dreamy butterflies
With dazzling colours powdered and soft glooms,
White, black and crimson stripes, and peacock eyes,
Or on chance flowers sit,
With idle effort plundering one by one
The nectaries of deepest-throated blooms.

Context

From *The Jewel Garden, 2004* | Monty Don (1955–)

We decided to make flowerbeds where the grass had been, without really knowing what we wanted them to do.

You might ask why flowers should do anything at all? But in a garden context is everything. No plant has meaning unless it relates to its neighbouring plants, hedges and trees, paths, walls or fences, surrounding buildings and even the quality of the light. Especially the light. What looks great under a Californian or Mediterranean sky can look stranded further north.

10 September

A Jewel Garden

From *Tales from the Arabian Nights' Entertainments, first English translation 1704–1717* | Translated by Rev. George Fyler Townsend (1814–1900)

The Story of Aladdin

He stopped in the garden to observe the trees, which were loaded with extraordinary fruit, of different colours on each tree. Some bore fruit entirely white and some clear and transparent as crystal; some pale red, and others deeper; some green, blue, and purple, and others yellow; in short, there was fruit of all colours. The white were pearls; the clear and transparent, diamonds; the deep red, rubies; the paler, ballas rubies; the green, emeralds; the blue, turquoises; the purple, amethysts; and the yellow, sapphires. Aladdin, ignorant of their value, would have preferred figs, or grapes, or pomegranates.

Evening

From *Wuthering Heights, 1847* | Emily Brontë (1818–1848)

On a mellow evening in September, I was coming from the
garden with a heavy basket of apples which I had been gathering.
It had got dusk, and the moon looked over the high wall of the
court, causing undefined shadows to lurk in the corners of the
numerous projecting portions of the building. I set my burden
on the house-steps by the kitchen-door, and lingered to rest, and
drew in a few more breaths of the soft, sweet air.

12 September

The Returning Traveller

From *Italian Villas and their Gardens, 1904* | Edith Wharton
(1862–1937)

The traveller returning from Italy, with his eyes and imagination
full of the ineffable Italian garden-magic, knows vaguely that
the enchantment exists; that he has been under its spell, and that
it is more potent, more enduring, more intoxicating to every
sense than the most elaborate and glowing effects of modern
horticulture; but he may not have found the key to the mystery.
Is it because the sky is bluer, because the vegetation is more
luxuriant? Our midsummer skies are almost as deep, our foliage
is as rich, and perhaps more varied; there are, indeed, not a few
resemblances between the North American summer climate and
that of Italy in spring and autumn.

Some of those who have fallen under the spell are inclined
to ascribe the Italian garden-magic to the effect of time; but,
wonder-working as this undoubtedly is, it leaves many beauties
unaccounted for. To seek the answer one must go deeper: the
garden must be studied in relation to the house, and both in
relation to the landscape.

Thoughts Upon Italian Gardens

From *Travels in France and Italy: Letter XXXI, 1771* | Tobias
Smollett (1721–1771)

He who loves the beauties of simple nature, and the charms of
neatness will seek for them in vain amidst the groves of Italy.
In the garden of the Villa Pinciana, there is a plantation of
four hundred pines, which the Italians view with rapture and
admiration: there is likewise a long walk, of trees extending from
the garden-gate to the palace; and plenty of shade, with alleys
and hedges in different parts of the ground: but the groves are
neglected; the walks are laid with nothing but common mould
or sand, black and dusty; the hedges are tall, thin and shabby; the
trees stunted; the open ground, brown and parched, has scarce
any appearance of verdure. The flat, regular alleys of evergreens
are cut into fantastic figures; the flower gardens embellished with thin
cyphers and flourished figures in box, while the flowers grow in rows
of earthen-pots, and the ground appears as dusky as if it was covered
with the cinders of a blacksmith's forge. The water, of which
there is great plenty, instead of being collected in large pieces, or
conveyed in little rivulets and streams to refresh the thirsty soil,
or managed so as to form agreeable cascades, is squirted from
fountains in different parts of the garden, through tubes little
bigger than common glyster-pipes. It must be owned indeed
that the fountains have their merit in the way of sculpture
and architecture; and that here is a great number of statues
which merit attention: but they serve only to encumber the
ground, and destroy that effect of rural simplicity, which our
gardens are designed to produce. In a word, here we see a variety
of walks and groves and fountains, a wood of four hundred pines,
a paddock with a few meagre deer, a flower-garden, an aviary, a
grotto, and a fish-pond; and in spite of all these particulars, it is,
in my opinion, a very contemptible garden, when compared to
that of Stowe in Buckinghamshire, or even to those of Kensington
and Richmond. The Italians understand, because they study, the
excellencies of art; but they have no idea of the beauties of nature.

Tom's Garden

From Agnes Grey, 1847 | Anne Brontë (1820–1849)

The garden was a large one, and tastefully laid out; besides several splendid dahlias, there were some other fine flowers still in bloom: but my companion would not give me time to examine them; I must go with him, across the wet grass, to a remote sequestered corner, the most important place in the grounds, because it contained his garden. There were two round beds, stocked with a variety of plants. In one there was a pretty little rose-tree. I paused to admire its lovely blossoms.

'Oh, never mind that!' said he, contemptuously. 'That's only *Mary Ann's* garden; look, THIS is mine.'

After I had observed every flower, and listened to a disquisition on every plant, I was permitted to depart, but first, with great pomp, he plucked a polyanthus and presented it to me, as one conferring a prodigious favour.

A Difference of Opinion

From *We Made a Garden, 1956* | Margery Fish (1892–1969)

In addition to roses and clematis, Walter had a deep passion for dahlias, the bigger, the brighter and the fleshier the better.

He bought a large collection from an expert almost as soon as we bought the house, and the first summer they enjoyed a secluded season in front of the hedge that separated us from the next house. There was no other place then in which to grow them, and I thought it was an admirable permanent home for them, a position all to themselves, with a hedge as background, but Walter felt they were being slighted by being put in the background and when I came to plant my terraced garden I was told to leave plenty of large spaces for the dahlias.

Unfortunately they were never labelled, so I had no idea what colours they were. Walter said they were all so lovely that it didn't matter. I held other views but was not clever enough to evolve a way of labelling them.

. . . .

The problem has been solved for me because I was never very successful in keeping tubers through the winter.

The Problem of Colour

From *Alice's Adventures in Wonderland, 1865* | Lewis Carroll
(1832–1898)

A large rose-tree stood near the entrance of the garden: the roses growing on it were white, but there were three gardeners at it, busily painting them red. Alice thought this a very curious thing, and she went nearer to watch them, and just as she came up to them she heard one of them say 'Look out now, Five! Don't go splashing paint over me like that!'

'I couldn't help it,' said Five, in a sulky tone. 'Seven jogged my elbow.'

On which Seven looked up and said 'That's right, Five! Always lay the blame on others!'

'*You'd* better not talk!' said Five. 'I heard the Queen say only yesterday you deserved to be beheaded.'

'What for?' said the one who had spoken first.

'That's none of *your* business, Two!' said Seven.

'Yes, it *is* his business!' said Five, 'and I'll tell him − it was for bringing the cook tulip-roots instead of onions.'

Seven flung down his brush, and had just begun 'Well, of all the unjust things —' when his eye chanced to fall upon Alice, as she stood watching them, and he checked himself suddenly: the others looked round also, and all of them bowed low.

'Would you tell me, please,' said Alice, a little timidly, 'why you are painting those roses?'

Five and Seven said nothing, but looked at Two. Two began in a low voice, 'Why the fact is, you see, Miss, this here ought to have been a *red* rose-tree, and we put a white one in by mistake; and, if the Queen was to find it out, we should all have our heads cut off, you know. So you see, Miss, we're doing our best, afore she comes, to —' At this moment Five, who had been anxiously looking across the garden, called out 'The Queen! The Queen!' and the three gardeners instantly threw themselves flat upon their faces.

The Garden at Evening

From *To the Lighthouse, 1927* | Virginia Woolf (1882–1941)

'It suddenly gets cold. The sun seems to give less heat,' she said, looking about her, for it was bright enough, the grass still a soft deep green, the house starred in its greenery with purple passion flowers, and rooks dropping cool cries from the high blue. But something moved, flashed, turned a silver wing in the air. It was September after all, the middle of September, and past six in the evening. So off they strolled down the garden in the usual direction, past the tennis lawn, past the pampas grass, to that break in the thick hedge, guarded by red hot pokers like braziers of clear burning coal, between which the blue waters of the bay looked bluer than ever.

I Remember

Thomas Hood (1799–1845)

I remember, I remember,
The house where I was born,
The little window where the sun
Came peeping in at morn;
He never came a wink too soon,
Nor brought too long a day,
But now, I often wish the night
Had borne my breath away!

I remember, I remember,
The roses, red and white,
The vi'lets, and the lily-cups,
Those flowers made of light!
The lilacs where the robin built,
And where my brother set
The laburnum on his birthday, –
The tree is living yet!

I remember, I remember,
Where I used to swing,
And thought the air must rush as fresh
To swallows on the wing;
My spirit flew in feathers then,
That is so heavy now,
And summer pools could hardly cool
The fever on my brow!

I remember, I remember,
The fir trees dark and high;
I used to think their slender tops
Were close against the sky:
It was a childish ignorance,
But now 'tis little joy
To know I'm farther off from heav'n
Than when I was a boy.

To be done in the Parterre and Flower Garden: The Advancing Cold

From *Kalendarium Hortense, 1664* | John Evelyn (1620–1706)

Bind now up your *Autumnal Flowers* and *Plants* to *Stakes*, to prevent sudden *Gusts*, which will else prostrate all you have so industriously raised.

The Cold now advancing, set such *Plants* as will not endure the *House* into the *Earth*; the Pots two or three *Inches* lower than the *surface* of some *Bed* under a *Southern* exposure. Then *cover* them with *Glasses*, having *cloathed* them first with sweet and dry *Moss*; but upon all *warm* and benign *emissions* of the *Sun*, and sweet *Showers*, give them *Air*, by taking off all that covers them. Thus you shall preserve your costly and precious *Marum Syriacum*, *Cistus's*, *Geranium nocte olens*, *Flos Cardinalis*, *Marcocs*, seedling *Arbutus's* (a very hardy plant when greater), choicest *Ranunculus's* and *Anemonies*, *Acacia Ægypt*, &c. Thus governing them till *April*. Secrets not till now divulged.

Note, that *Cats* will eat and destroy your *Marum Syriacum*, if they can come at it; therefore guard it with a *Furse* or *Holy-branch*.

A Bonnet-Shop

From *Under the Greenwood Tree, 1872* | Thomas Hardy (1840–1928)

A group of hollyhocks in flower, round which a crowd of
butterflies had gathered like female idlers round a bonnet-shop.

21 September

The Castle Garden

From *The Princess and the Goblin, 1870–1872* | George MacDonald
(1824–1905)

22 September

PRINCESS IRENE AND HER FATHER THE KING WALK IN THE GARDEN:

The garden was a very lovely place. Being upon a mountainside
there were parts in it where the rocks came through in great
masses, and all immediately about them remained quite wild.
Tufts of heather grew upon them, and other hardy mountain
plants and flowers, while near them would be lovely roses and
lilies, and all pleasant garden flowers. This mingling of the wild
mountain with the civilized garden was very quaint, and it was
impossible for any number of gardeners to make such a garden
look formal and stiff.

Against one of these rocks was a garden seat, shadowed from the
afternoon sun by the overhanging of the rock itself. There was a
little winding path up to the top of the rock, and on top another
seat; but they sat on the seat at its foot because the sun was hot;
and there they talked together of many things.

To Autumn

1820 | John Keats (1795–1821)

I

Season of mists and mellow fruitfulness,
    Close bosom-friend of the maturing sun;
Conspiring with him how to load and bless
    With fruit the vines that round the thatch-eves run;
To bend with apples the moss'd cottage-trees,
    And fill all fruit with ripeness to the core;
        To swell the gourd, and plump, the hazel shells
    With a sweet kernel; to set budding more,
And still more, later flowers for the bees,
Until they think warm days will never cease,
    For Summer has o'er-brimmed their clammy cells.

II

Who hath not seen thee oft amid thy store?
    Sometimes whoever seeks abroad may find
Thee sitting careless on a granary floor,
    Thy hair soft-lifted by the winnowing wind;
Or on a half-reap'd furrow sound asleep,
    Drows'd with the fume of poppies, while thy hook
        Spares the next swathe and all its twined flowers:
And sometimes like a gleaner thou dost keep
    Steady thy laden head across a brook;
    Or by a cyder-press, with patient look,
        Thou watchest the last oozing hours by hours.

III
Where are the songs of Spring? Ay, where are they?
Think not of them, thou hast thy music too, −
While barred clouds bloom the soft-dying day,
And touch the stubble-plains with rosy hue;
Then in a wilful choir the small gnats mourn
Among the river sallows, borne aloft
Or sinking as the light wind lives or dies;
And full-grown lambs loud bleat from hilly bourn;
Hedge-crickets sing; and now with treble soft
The red-breast whistles from a garden-croft;
And gathering swallows twitter in the skies.

Playing Millinery

From *Onward and Upward in the Garden*, 1979 | Katharine S. White (1892–1977)

THE NEW YORKER, SEPTEMBER 24, 1960

Most people do not pick their flowering shrubs, but we always did. I can remember the succession of flowering branches, plucked by the adults of the household and arranged by them in a tall gray Chinese jar, in our gold-and-green parlour. My sister and I and our friends had a game we played with the shrubbery. It was called Millinery. All the little girls in the neighborhood would bring to our lawn their broad-brimmed straw school hats, which, because they were Boston girls' hats, only had plain ribbon bands for decoration. Then each of us would trim her straw with blossoms from the shrubs. There was a wide choice of trimmings – forsythia, Japanese crab, Japanese quince, mock orange, flowering almond, lilac, hawthorn, bridal wreath, weigelas, deutzia, with its tiny white bells, and, in June, altheas and shrub roses. We were not allowed to pick the rhododendrons or azaleas, but nothing else was forbidden. When our flowery concoctions were completed, we put them on our heads and proudly paraded into the house to show them off to our elders; it seems to me now that we must have made quite a gay sight. By dusk the trimmings were dead, and the next day we could start all over again.

Absence

From *The House of Seven Gables, 1851* | Nathaniel Hawthorne
(1804–1864)

The growth of the garden seemed to have got quite out of bounds; the weeds had taken advantage of Phoebe's absence, and the long-continued rain, to run rampant over the flowers and kitchen-vegetables. Maule's Well had overflowed its stone-border, and made a pool of formidable breadth in that corner of the garden.

The impression of the whole scene was that of a spot, where no human foot had left its print, for many preceding days.

25 September

The Omnipotent Magician

From *The Task*, 1785 | William Cowper (1731–1800)

BOOK III, THE GARDEN, LINES 765–789

Lo, he comes!

Th' omnipotent magician, Brown, appears!
Down falls the venerable pile, th' abode
Of our forefathers — a grave whisker'd race,
But tasteless. Springs a palace in its stead,
But in a distant spot; where more expos'd,
It may enjoy th' advantage of the north,
And aguish east, till time shall have transform'd
Those naked acres to a shelt'ring grove.
He speaks. The lake in front becomes a lawn;
Woods vanish, hills subside, and vallies rise:
And streams, as if created for his use,
Pursue the track of his directing wand,
Sinuous or straight, now rapid and now slow,
Now murm'ring soft, now roaring in cascades —
Even as he bids! The enraptured owner smiles.
'Tis finish'd, and yet, finish'd as it seems,
Still wants a grace, the loveliest it could show,
A mine to satisfy th' enormous cost.
Drain'd to the last poor item of his wealth,
He sighs, departs, and leaves th' accomplish'd plan
That he has touch'd and retouch'd, many a long day
Labour'd, and many a night pursu'd in dreams,
Just when it meets his hopes, and proves the heav'n
He wanted, for a wealthier to enjoy!

For Good Landscape Design

From *A Letter to Rev. Thomas Dyer, 1775* | Lancelot 'Capability' Brown (1716–1783)

A perfect knowledge of the country and the objects in it, whether natural or artificial, and infinite delicacy in the planting etc., so much Beauty depending on the size of trees and the colour of their leaves to produce the effect of light and shade.

27 September

A Wish

Richard Owen Cambridge (1717–1802)

The poet Richard Owen Cambridge is believed to have
remarked of 'Capability' Brown that:

'I hope to die before him, so I may see heaven before it
is improved!'

His wish was not granted as 'Capability' Brown died in
1783 and would have had ample time to improve the
landscape of heaven before the poet's arrival.

28 September

Rain and Wind

From *The Portrait of a Lady, 1881* | Henry James (1843–1916)

The autumn twilight gathered in, and from her place Isabel could see the rain, which had now begun in earnest, washing the cold-looking lawn and the wind shaking the great trees.

Gathering Fruit

From *Five Hundred Points of Good Husbandry, 1557, 1573*

Thomas Tusser (1524–1580)

Gathering of fruit.

The Moone in the wane, gather fruit for to last,
   but winter fruit gather when Michael is past;
Though michers that love not to buy nor to crave,
   makes some gather sooner, else few for to have.

Too early gathering is not best.

Fruit gathred too timely wil taste of the wood,
   wil shrink and be bitter, and seldome proove good
So fruit that is shaken, or beat off a tree,
   with brusing in falling, soone faultie wil bee.

OCTOBER

Stately Trees and Grassy Banks

Careless Grace

From *The Garden that I Love, 1894* | Alfred Austin (1835–1913)

Autumn knows the art of gardening to perfection, possessing the secret of careless grace even beyond the Spring. There is an orderly negligence about autumnal forms and colours no other season can match. Even to the garden proper, the cultivated plots of man, Autumn adds such wonderful touches of happy accident that, when it comes, a wise man leaves his garden alone and allows it to fade, and wane, and slowly, pathetically, pass away, without any effort to hinder or conceal the decay. Indeed, it would be worthwhile having a cultivated garden if only to see what Autumn does with it.

1 October

Falling Leaves

From *The Man of Property, 1906* | John Galsworthy (1867–1933)

He decided to commence with the Botanical Gardens, where he had already made so many studies, and chose the little artificial pond, sprinkled now with an autumn shower of red and yellow leaves, for though the gardeners longed to sweep them off, they could not reach them with their brooms. The rest of the gardens they swept bare enough, removing every morning Nature's rain of leaves; piling them in heaps, whence from slow fires rose the sweet, acrid smoke that, like the cuckoo's note for spring, the scent of lime trees for the summer, is the true emblem of the fall. The gardeners' tidy souls could not abide the gold and green and russet pattern on the grass. The gravel paths must lie unstained, ordered, methodical, without knowledge of the realities of life, nor of that slow and beautiful decay which flings crowns underfoot to star the earth with fallen glories, whence, as the cycle rolls, will leap again wild spring.

Thus each leaf that fell was marked from the moment when it fluttered a good-bye and dropped, slow turning, from its twig.

But on that little pond the leaves floated in peace, and praised Heaven with their hues, the sunlight haunting over them.

Leaves

From *Cuttings from My Garden Notebooks*, 1997 | Graham Stuart
Thomas (1909–2003)

Nine-tenths of the garden's yearly beauty is from leaves, yet
we accord our fullest attention to flowers. Leaves are not only
a background to flowers but an integral part of garden design
and management; the evergreen shrubs control our views,
and without ground-covering plants we should have to resort
to hoeing or hand weeding, or even digging. Now, I have no
objection to digging: it is a satisfying and excellent exercise; but if
one is to have a well filled garden the spaces needing digging will
not be great, and the lowly spreading plants will resent it.

Careful choice of plants with due regard to their leaves will
be found to accentuate perspective if it is borne in mind that
larger, glossy-textured leaves should be placed to the fore, with
small, matt leaves farther away. The same applies to the tints of
the leaves, using the bright, light greens in front with dull and
sombre greens beyond.

3 October

Two Gardens

Walter de la Mare (1873–1956)

Two gardens see! – this, of enchanted flowers,
Strange to the eye, and more than earthly-sweet;
Small rivulets running, song-reëchoing bowers;
And green-walled pathways which, ere parting, meet;
And there a lion-like sun in heaven's delight
Breathes plenitude from dayspring to the night.

The other: – walls obscure, and chaces of trees,
Ilex and yew, and dream-enticing dark,
Hid pools, moths, creeping odours, silentness,
Luna its deity, and its watchword, *Hark!*
A still and starry mystery, wherein move
Phantoms of ageless wonder and of love.

Two gardens for two children – in one mind:
But ah, how seldom open now their gates I find!

Beauty

From *Home and Garden, 1900* | Gertrude Jekyll (1843–1932)

It always seems to me that one of the things most worth doing about a garden is to try to make every part of it beautiful; not the pleasure garden only, but some of the rough accessories also, so that no place is unsightly.

Gardens at Night

From *The Back of the North Wind, 1868–1871* | George MacDonald
(1824–1905)

THE NORTH WIND TAKES DIAMOND ALONG THE RIVER:

Sometimes she would leave the river and sweep across a clover-
field. The bees were all at home, and the clover was asleep. Then
she would return and follow the river. It grew wider and wider
as it went. Now the armies of wheat and of oats would hang over
its rush from the opposite banks; now the willows would dip low
branches in its still waters; and now it would lead them through
stately trees and grassy banks into a lovely garden, where the
roses and lilies were asleep, the tender flowers quite folded up,
and only a few wide-awake and sending out their life in sweet,
strong odours.

6 October

Ravenshoe Hall in 1831

From *Ravenshoe, 1861* | Henry Kingsley (1830–1876)

In front of the west wing, a terraced flower-garden goes step by
step towards the stream, till the smooth-shaven lawns almost
mingle with the wild ferny heather turf of the park, where the
dappled deer browse, and the rabbit runs to and fro busily. On
the north, towards the sea, there are no gardens; but a noble
gravel terrace, divided from the park only by a deep rampart,
runs along beneath the windows; and to the east the deer-
park stretches away till lawn and glade are swallowed up in the
encroaching woodland.

Leaf-mould

From *Gardening for the Ignorant, 1912* | Mrs Earle (1836–1925) and Ethel Case

Every garden should have some place in which to make a store for leaf-mould. The best place is against a fence or wall, behind some shrubs or in the field. A space should be divided by some slats of wood into two compartments, like stalls in a stable, all garden refuse that is not full of seeds or roots of weeds can be thrown into the first stall, together with all the leaves you can collect, and the sweepings from the drive and gravel paths, and dead flowers from the house. When this heap is as high as the palings will hold it, it must be turned over to the other stall and will be ready, when quite decayed and rotted to the consistency of mould, to use for potting or for putting on the garden beds, and the first stall can be filled by degrees as before.

8 October

Digging

Edward Thomas (1878–1917)

To-day I think
Only with scents, — scents dead leaves yield,
And bracken, and wild carrot's seed,
And the square mustard field;

Odours that rise
When the spade wounds the root of tree,
Rose, currant, raspberry, or goutweed,
Rhubarb or celery;

The smoke's smell, too,
Flowing from where a bonfire burns
The dead, the waste, the dangerous,
And all to sweetness turns.

It is enough
To smell, to crumble the dark earth,
While the robin sings over again
Sad songs of Autumn mirth.

The Goose Tree

From *Gossip in a Library: Gerard's Herbal, 1891* | Edmund Gosse
(1849–1928)

Our good herbalist, however, cannot get through his sixteen
hundred accurate and solemn pages without one slip. After
accompanying him dutifully so far, we double up with
uncontrollable laughter on p1587, for here begins the chapter
which treats 'of the Goose Tree, Barnacle Tree, or the Tree
bearing Geese'. But even here the habit of genuine observation
clings to him. The picture represents a group of stalked barnacles
– those shrimps fixed by their antennae, which modern science,
I believe, calls Lepas anatifera; by the side of these stands a little
goose, and the suggestion of course is that the latter has slipped
out of the former, although the draughtsman has been far too
conscientious to represent the occurrence. Yet the letterpress is
confident that in the north parts of Scotland there are trees on
which grow white shells, which ripen, and then, opening, drop
little living geese into the waves below. Gerard himself avers that
from Guernsey and Jersey he brought home with him to London
shells, like limpets, containing little feathery objects, 'which, no
doubt, were the fowls called Barnacles'. It is almost needless to say
that these objects really were the plumose and flexible cirri which
the barnacles throw out to catch their food with, and which lie,
like a tiny feather-brush, just within the valves of the shell, when
the creature is dead. Gerard was plainly unable to refuse credence
to the mass of evidence which presented itself to him on this
subject, yet he closes with a hint that this seems rather a 'fabulous
breed' of geese.

With the Barnacle Goose Tree the Herbal proper closes, in these quaint words:

'And thus having, through God's assistance, discoursed somewhat at large of grasses, herbs, shrubs, trees and mosses, and certain excrescences of the earth, with other things moe, incident to the history thereof, we conclude, and end our present volume with this wonder of England. For the which God's name be ever honoured and praised'.

And so, at last, the Goose Tree receives the highest sanction.

The Head Gardener

From *The Small House at Allington, 1862–1864* | Anthony Trollope
(1815–1882)

The entire garden belonging to the Small House, was in the
hands of Hopkins, the head gardener to the Great House; and it
was so simply for this reason, that Mrs Dale could not afford to
keep a gardener herself. A working lad, at ten shillings a week,
who cleaned the knives and shoes, and dug the ground, was
the only male attendant on the three ladies. But Hopkins, the
head gardener of Allington, who had men under him, was as
widely awake to the lawn and the conservatory of the humbler
establishment as he was to the grapery, peach-walls, and terraces
of the grander one. In his eyes it was all one place. The Small
House belonged to his master, as indeed did the very furniture
within it; and it was lent, not let, to Mrs Dale. Hopkins, perhaps,
did not love Mrs Dale, seeing that he owed her no duty as one
born a Dale. The two young ladies he did love, and also snubbed
in a very peremptory way sometimes. To Mrs Dale he was coldly
civil, always referring to the squire if any direction worthy of
special notice as concerning the garden was given to him.

. . . .

Hopkins appeared at the parlour window, and signified his desire
for a conference.

'You must come round,' said Lily. 'It's too cold for the window to
be opened. I always like to get him into the house, because he feels
himself a little abashed by the chairs and tables; or, perhaps, it is the
carpet that is too much for him. Out on the gravel-walks he is such a
terrible tyrant, and in the greenhouse he almost tramples upon one!'

Hopkins, when he did appear at the parlour door, seemed by his
manner to justify Lily's discretion. He was not at all masterful in
his tone or bearing, and seemed to pay to the chairs and tables all
the deference which they could have expected.

Gardens and Gardeners

From *Cyrus's Garden or The Quincunx, 1658* | Sir Thomas Browne
(1605–1682)

If Paradise were planted the third day of the creation, as wiser divinity concludeth, the nativity thereof was too early for horoscopy: gardens were before gardeners, but some hours after the earth.

An October Garden

Christina Rossetti (1830–1894)

In my Autumn garden I was fain
    To mourn among my scattered roses;
    Alas for that last rosebud which uncloses
To Autumn's languid sun and rain
When all the world is on the wane!
    Which has not felt the sweet constraint of June,
    Nor heard the nightingale in tune.

Broad-faced asters by my garden walk,
    You are but coarse compared with roses:
    More choice, more dear that rosebud which uncloses,
Faint-scented, pinched, upon its stalk,
That least and last which cold winds balk;
    A rose it is tho' least and last of all,
    A rose to me tho' at the fall.

Controlled Wilderness

From *In the Eye of the Garden, 1993* | Mirabel Osler (1925–2016)

Controlled wilderness is hard work. Careless gardening is
not what it seems. Cow parsley wasn't in our garden through
negligence but because, when sitting by the stream, we wanted
to see the brazenly pink rose, 'Zéphirine Drouhin', through
the creamy lace of the flowers. The whole choreography of our
garden meant that keeping it to the right degree of wilderness
needed stern application; the link between harmony and
disintegration is a fine one. Our method of gardening appeared
haphazard, with tulips growing among long grass, but the
flounces of the roses trailing on the ground kept us in bondage all
summer long, needing to sickle round the frilly bits before nettles
and grass obliterated their hems. It was arduous; mowing became
a co-operative obligation, when I would hoist up the straggles
of roses on the prongs of a hay fork while Michael pushed the
mower beneath.

The tumbled disarray which some of our best gardeners achieve,
with what looks like artless genius, has form. Ask them, and they
admit that those parts of the garden which look so spontaneous
need painstaking attention, defined and inspired.

A Great Surprise

From *Tom's Midnight Garden, 1958* | Philippa Pearce (1920–2006)

WHEN THE CLOCK STRUCK THIRTEEN:

Tom opened the door wide and let in the moonlight. It flooded in, as bright as daylight – the white daylight that comes before the full rising of the sun. The illumination was perfect, but Tom did not at once turn to see what it showed him on the clock-face. Instead he took a step forward on the doorstep. He was staring, at first in surprise, then with indignation, at what he saw outside. That they should have deceived him – lied to him – like this! They had said, 'It's not worth your while going out at the back, Tom.' So carelessly had they described it: 'A sort of back-yard, very poky, with rubbish bins. Really, there's nothing to see.'

Nothing . . . Only this: a great lawn where flower-beds bloomed; a towering fir-tree, and thick, beetle-browed yews that humped their shapes down two sides of the lawn; on the third side to the right, a greenhouse almost the size of a real house; from each corner of the lawn, a path that twisted away to some other depths of garden, with other trees.

Altering Beds

From *Pot-Pourri from a Surrey Garden, 1897* | Mrs Earle
(1836–1925)

It is a very good plan, when you want to cut a new bed or alter
the shape of an old one, to shuffle along the wet dewy grass on an
October morning – and this leaves a mark which enables you very
well to judge the size, shape, and proportion – before you begin
to cut your beds out.

The Last Rose of Summer

Thomas Moore (1779–1852)

'Tis the last rose of summer,
   Left blooming alone;
All her lovely companions
   Are faded and gone;
No flower of her kindred,
   No rosebud is nigh,
To reflect back her blushes
   Or give sigh for sigh!

I'll not leave thee, thou lone one!
   To pine on the stem;
Since the lovely are sleeping,
   Go sleep thou with them;
Thus kindly I scatter
   Thy leaves o'er the bed
Where thy mates of the garden
   Lie scentless and dead.

So soon may I follow,
   When friendships decay,
And from love's shining circle
   The gems drop away!
When true hearts lie wither'd,
   And fond ones are flown,
Oh! who would inhabit
   This bleak world alone?

The Vegetable or Kitchen Garden: Tubers

From *The Beeton Book of Garden Management, 1862* | Samuel
Orchart Beeton (1831–1877)

The tubers are now at maturity. Dig them up and store for the
winter, so as to protect them from frost. The three-pronged
potato-fork, with broad tines, rounded and blunt at the points, is
a well-known implement. It is usual, where the haulm is strong,
to cut off the tops, and by inserting the fork under the whole
plant, turn the whole up in a mass, the potatoes being collected
after the digger in baskets; they may either be stored in a suitable
room, or stowed away in pits in open ground, properly drained
and covered, first with a layer of earth, then with a thatching of
clean straw, and then with soil sufficiently thick to protect them
from the severest frosts.

A Charming Seat

From *The Posthumous Papers of the Pickwick Club,*
1836–1837 | Charles Dickens (1812–1870)

There was a bower at the farther end, with honeysuckle,
jessamine, and creeping plants — one of those sweet retreats
which humane men erect for the accommodation of spiders.

19 October

A Scarecrow

From *Heath Robinson: How to Make a Garden,* 1938 | W. Heath
Robinson (1872–1944) | Written by K. R. G. Brown (1895–1940)

An essential feature of every kitchen-garden is a scarecrow,
adolescent vegetables having an irresistible attraction for birds of
weak moral fibre. The more life-like the scarecrow, obviously,
the greater its efficiency as a frightener of freebooting fowls; but
any old Gent's Spring Suiting, stuffed with rook's feathers and
surmounted by a disused bowler, will suffice for all ordinary
occasions, such refinements as socks and a wrist-watch not
being really necessary. Gardeners who have no old clothes,
other than those they are wearing, will find that octogenarian
uncles in reduced circumstances are usually willing, for a small
consideration, to take over the scarecrow's duties.

A Democratic Fruit

From *Pleasant Talk about Fruits, Flowers and Farming, 1859, 1874* | Henry Ward Beecher (1813–1887)

The apple tree is homely; but it is also hardy, and not only in respect to climate. It is almost indifferent to soil and exposure. We should as soon think of coddling an oak tree or a chestnut; we should as soon think of shielding from the winter white pine or hemlock, as an apple tree. If there is a lot too steep for the plow or too rocky for tools, the farmer dedicates it to an apple orchard. Nor do the trees betray his trust. Yet, the apple loves the meadows. It will thrive in sandy loams, and adapt itself to the toughest clay. It will bear as much dryness as a mullein stalk, and as much wet, almost, as a willow. In short, it is a genuine democrat. It can be poor, while it loves to be rich; it can be plain, although it prefers to be ornate; it can be neglected, notwithstanding it welcomes attention. But, whether neglected, abused, or abandoned, it is able to take care of itself, and to be fruitful of excellences. That is what I call being democratic.

21 October

Some Trees of the Fruit Garden

From *The Gardener's Manual containing Practical Instructions for the Cultivation and Management of the Flower, the Fruit and the Kitchen Garden: Hot House, Green House and Conservatory. Adapted to Small or Large Gardens, eighth edition, 1843* | Anon

The Chestnut is more a tree of the shrubbery than of the fruit garden, and when planted may be left to the care of Dame Nature.

Filberts may occupy with advantage the border near the outer edge of the garden to form a low screen, as they should not be allowed to attain any great height. They should be pruned annually, taking out all dead wood. The fruit should be suffered to hang till it is ready to drop out of the husk, and the bud end turns white, or it will not keep well, as the kernels shrivel up when gathered.

Medlars are not held in much estimation, but sometimes occupy a place in the shrubbery.

The Mulberry should stand in the lawn, or at least have a glass-plat under it, as the fruit is never so good as when it hangs on the tree till it is sufficiently ripe to fall, and to fall on mould would spoil the fruit.

Quinces are not fit for the table; they are used as a flavour with apples, and make an elegant preserve or marmalade.

Walnuts are more fit for the park than for the garden or orchard, but they are by no means unbecoming appendages to the pleasure-ground.

Shakespeare's Mulberry Tree

From *Life of Johnson, 1791* | James Boswell (1740–1795)

MR BOSWELL DINES WITH MRS GASTREL:

I was not informed till afterwards that Mrs Gastrel's husband was the clergyman who, while he lived at Stratford-upon-Avon, where he was the proprietor of Shakespeare's garden, with Gothic barbarity, cut down his mulberry-tree, and, as Dr Johnson told me, did it to vex his neighbours. His lady, I have reason to believe, on the same authority, participated in the guilt of what the enthusiasts of our immortal bard deem almost a species of sacrilege.

To be done in the Parterre and Flower Garden: Anemonies and Autumn Leaves

From *Kalendarium Hortense, 1664* | John Evelyn (1620–1706)

You may plant some *Anemonies:* especially the *Tenuifolia's,* and *Ranunculus's* in fresh *sandish Earth,* taken from under the *Turf,* but lay richer *Mould* at the *bottom* of the *Bed,* which the *Fibres* may reach, but not to touch the main *Roots,* which are to be cover'd with the *natural Earth* two Inches deep: and so soon as they appear, secure them with *Mats* or dry *Straw,* from the *Winds* and *Frosts,* giving them *air* in all benign *Intervals,* if possible *once* a day.

Plant now your choice *Tulips,* &c. which you fear'd to *interre* at the beginning of *September;* they will be more secure, and forward enough: but plant them in *natural Earth* somewhat *impoverished* with very fine *Sand;* else they will soon loose their *variegations;* some more *rich Earth* may lie at the bottom, within reach of the *Fibres* (as above).

Sweep, and cleanse your *Walks,* and all other *Places,* from *Autumn Leaves* fallen, lest the *Worms* draw them into their *Holes,* and foul your *Gardens,* &c.

To Penshurst

1616 | Ben Jonson (1572–1637)

LINES 1–14

Thou art not, PENSHURST, built to envious show,
    Of touch, or marble; nor canst boast a row
Of polish'd pillars, or roofe of gold:
    Thou hast no lantherne, whereof tales are told;
Or stayre, or courts, but stand'st an ancient pile,
    And these grudg'd at, art reverenc'd the while.
Thou joy'st in better markes, of soyle, of ayre,
    Of wood, of water: therein thou art faire.
Thou hast thy walkes for health, as well as sport:
    Thy *Mount*, to which the *Dryads* doe resort,
Where PAN, and BACCHUS their high feasts have made,
    Beneath the broad beech, and the chest-nut shade;
That taller tree, which of a nut was set,
    At his great birth, where all the *Muses* met.

Refreshing the Fainting Naiads

From *The Expedition of Humphry Clinker, vol III, 1771* | Tobias Smollett (1721–1771)

MATT TAKES STEPS TO PUT MR BAYNARD'S AFFAIRS, AND HIS GARDEN, IN ORDER:

To Dr Lewis

Oct. 26

Dear Dick,

With Baynard's good leave, I ordered the gardener to turn the rivulet into its old channel, to refresh the fainting Naiads, who had so long languished among mouldring roots, withered leaves, and dry pebbles. – The shrubbery is condemned to extirpation; and the pleasure-ground will be restored to its original use of corn-field and pasture. – Orders are given for rebuilding the walls of the garden at the back of the house, and for planting clumps of firs, intermingled with beech and chestnut, which is now quite exposed to the surly blasts that come from that quarter.

. . . .

Yours,

Matt. Bramble

Front Yards

From *Old Time Gardens, 1901* | Alice Morse Earle (1851–1911)

The word yard, not generally applied now to any enclosure of elegant cultivation, comes from the same root as the word garden.

. . . .

This front yard was an English fashion derived from the forecourt so strongly advised by Gervayse Markham (an interesting old English writer on floriculture and husbandry), and found in front of many a yeoman's house, and many a more pretentious house as well in Markham's day. Forecourts were common in England until the middle of the eighteenth century, and may still be seen. The forecourt gave privacy to the house even when in the centre of a town. Its readoption is advised with handsome dwellings in England, where ground-space is limited, – and why not in America, too?

The front yard was sacred to the best beloved, or at any rate the most honored, garden flowers of the house mistress, and was preserved by its fences from inroads of cattle, which then wandered at their will and were not housed, or even enclosed at night. The flowers were often of scant variety, but were those deemed the gentlefolk of the flower world.

Coloured Lilies

From *The Second Book of the English Husbandman, 1613*

Gervase Markham (c.1568–1637)

If you would have your Lillyes of a purple colour, you shall steepe
your seedes in the Lees of red wine, and that will change their
complexion, and also you shall water the Plants with the same
Lees likewise: if you will have them scarlet red, you shall put
Vermillion or Cynaber betweene the rinde and the small heads
growing about the roote: if you would have then blew, you shall
dissolve Azure or Byse betweene the rinde and the heads, if yellow
Orpment, if greene Verdigreace, and thus any other colour.

Quality and Variety

From *Aristocrats of the Garden, 1917* | Ernest Henry 'Chinese' Wilson
(1876–1930)

My plea is for quality and variety, yet I find no pleasure in a garden crammed with a thousand-and-one things just because they have different names. I hate to see a private garden emulate a botanic garden to the exclusion of every consideration but wealth in variety. As a matter of fact I know of nothing more depressing than the average botanic garden with its rows of beds and army of prominent labels. It suggests too much a popular cemetery. No, with variety I want quality and I want each plant to be given the amount of air and food necessary for its full development. Robust health is ever inspiring to look upon. The size of a garden rules quantity but not quality. If in the garden there be room for one plant only then would I have this plant the most beautiful that can flourish there, and I would infinitely rather have a healthful, flourishing specimen of a common thing than an unhappy merely existing example of the rarest known plant, for in health and vigour beauty can always be found.

29 October

The Ruins of the Palace

From *Quentin Durward, 1823* | Sir Walter Scott (1731–1832)

Its remains run along a beautiful terrace overhanging the river
Loire, which had been formerly laid out with a succession of
steps, highly ornamented with statues, descending from one
terrace to another, until the very verge of the river was attained.
All this architectural decoration, with its accompanying parterres
of rich flowers and exotic shrubs, had, many years since, given
place to the more profitable scene of the vine-dresser's labours;
yet the remains, too massive to be destroyed, are still visible,
and, with the various artificial slopes and levels of the high bank,
bear perfect evidence how actively Art had been employed to
decorate Nature.

Few of these scenes are now left in perfection; for the fickleness
of fashion has accomplished in England the total change which
devastation and popular fury have produced in the French
pleasure-grounds.

General Directions

From *New Principles of Gardening, 1728* | Batty Langley (1696–1751)

I. That the grand Front of a Building lie open upon an elegant Lawn or Plain of Grass, adorn'd with beautiful Statues, (of which hereafter in their Place,) terminated on its Sides with open Groves.

II. That grand Avenues be planted from such large open Plains, with a Breadth proportionable to the Building, as well as to its Length of View.

III. That Views in Gardens be as extensive as possible.

IV. That such Walks, whose Views cannot be extended, terminate in Woods, Forests, misshapen Rocks, strange Precipices, Mountains, old Ruins, grand Buildings, &c.

V. That no regular Ever-Greens, &c. be planted in any Part of an open Plain or Parterre.

VI. That no Borders be made, or Scroll-Work cut, in any such Lawn or plain Parterre; for the Grandeur of those beautiful Carpets consists in their native Plainness.

VII. That all Gardens be grand, beautiful, and natural.
[There follow thirty more Directions.]

NOVEMBER

Leaves Circling Down

The Cottage Garden Triumphs

From *English Gardens, 1944* | Harry Roberts (1871–1946)

In the present century Britain has been involved in two great wars, conducted on novel lines, with novel weapons; the total effect of which on gardening in this country is bound to be immense. Already one sees a great reduction in the number of large gardens in private hands. The cultivation of flowers, except on the smallest scale, is discouraged, and large estates all over the country are being split up for building development. After the war, nearly all gardens in private hands will be essentially villa gardens or cottage gardens. We shall then see who among us are real gardeners.

. . . .

The future of the English garden is doubtful. Everything depends on whether the common man becomes vocal and assertive, or whether with his traditional modesty he leaves everything to be decided by 'leaders' who claim to know what is best for him. The findings of the recent Mass-observation enquiry on Housing into the real desires and aspirations of various groups of working people, establish the fact that although a number of the 'observed' were unaccustomed to visualise a world in which they had any right of choice, over eighty per cent of the total pictured their ideal home as a small convenient house 'with a garden.' Should this bit of democracy realise, the English cottage garden will have come into its own.

The Finer Points of Gardening

From *Letters from a Citizen of the World to his Friends in the East, 1762* | Oliver Goldsmith (1728–1774)

Extract: Letter XXX

From Lien Chi Altangi, to the care of Fipsihi, resident in Moscow, to be forwarded by the Russian caravan to Fum Hoam, first president of the ceremonial academy at Pekin in China.

The English have not yet brought the art of gardening to the same perfection with the Chinese, but have lately begun to imitate them: Nature is now followed with greater assiduity than formerly; the trees are suffered to shoot out into the utmost luxuriance; the streams, no longer forced from their native beds, are permitted to wind along the valleys: spontaneous flowers take place of the finished parterre, and the enamelled meadow of the shaven green.

Yet still the English are far behind us in this charming art; their designers have not yet attained a power of uniting instruction with beauty. A European will scarcely conceive my meaning, when I say that there is scarce a garden in China which does not contain some fine moral, couched under the general design, where one is not taught wisdom as he walks, and feels the force of some noble truth, or delicate precept resulting from the disposition of the groves, streams or grottos.

Brentham

From *Lothair, 1870* | Benjamin Disraeli (1804–1881)

It was an Italian palace of freestone; vast, ornate, and in
scrupulous condition; its spacious and graceful chambers filled
with treasures of art, and rising itself from statued and stately
terraces. At their foot spread a gardened domain of considerable
extent, bright with flowers, dim with coverts of rare shrubs, and
musical with fountains. Its limit reached a park, with timber
such as the midland counties only can produce. The fallow deer
trooped among its ferny solitudes and gigantic oaks; but, beyond
the waters of the broad and winding lake, the scene became more
savage, and the eye caught the dark forms of the red deer on some
jutting mount, shrinking with scorn from communion with his
gentler brethren.

3 November

Flowers and Italian Gardens

From *Italian Villas and their Gardens, 1904* | Edith Wharton
(1862–1937)

Though it is an exaggeration to say that there are no flowers in
Italian gardens, yet to enjoy and appreciate the Italian garden-
craft one must always bear in mind that it is independent of
floriculture.

The Italian garden does not exist for its flowers; its flowers exist
for it; they are a late and infrequent adjunct to its beauties, a
parenthetical grace counting only as one more touch in the
general effect of enchantment. This is no doubt partly explained
by the difficulty of cultivating any but spring flowers in so
hot and dry a climate, and the result has been a wonderful
development of the more permanent effects to be obtained from
the three other factors in garden-composition – marble, water
and perennial verdure – and the achievement, by their skilful
blending, of a charm independent of the seasons.

Filling the Cracks in Paving

From *In Your Garden, 1951* | Vita Sackville-West (1892–1962)

From an article in The Observer, November 5, 1949:

The first essential is that it is something that does not mind being walked upon. There was once a play called *Boots and Doormats,* which divided people into two categories: those who like to trample and those who enjoy being trampled. To-day, in modern jargon, I suppose they would be called tramplers and tramplees; I prefer boots and doormats as an expression of this fundamental truth. Many big boots will walk down a paved path, and there are some meek doormats prepared to put up with such gruff treatment. The creeping thymes really enjoy being walked on, and will crawl and crawl, spreading gradually into rivulets and pools of green, like water slowly trickling, increasing in volume as it goes, until they have filled up all the cracks and crevices. The thymes are the true standby for anybody who wants to carpet a paved path.

5 November

The Garden at Prospect Cottage

From *Modern Nature, 1991* | Derek Jarman (1942–1994)

MONDAY 6 NOVEMBER, 1989

A still, frosty morning – sun bright on the glittering shingle, not a cloud in the sky and very cold. Well wrapped I walk to the beach.

I love the mornings here – up with the sunshine, cups of coffee, steaming porridge and toast. The quiet is overwhelming after the snarling traffic of the Charing Cross Road. Only a year on, the garden looks as if it has been here as long as the house.

Now the flowers are dead; the multi-coloured flints, and the bright red bricks ground by the waves give it a friendly appearance.

It isn't a gloomy garden, its circles and squares have humour – a fairy ring for troglodytic pixies – the stones a notation for long-forgotten music, an ancestral round to which I add a few notes each morning.

The Trouble with Bulbs

From *The Diary of a Provincial Lady, 1930* | E. M. Delafield
(1890–1943)

November 7th. – Plant the indoor bulbs. Just as I am in the middle of them, Lady Boxe calls. I say, untruthfully, how nice to see her, and beg her to sit down while I just finish the bulbs. Lady B. makes determined attempt to sit down in armchair where I have already placed two bulb-bowls and the bag of charcoal, is headed off just in time, and takes the sofa.

Do I know, she asks, how very late it is for indoor bulbs? September, really, or even October, is the time. Do I know that the only really reliable firm for hyacinths is Somebody of Haarlem? Cannot catch the name of the firm, which is Dutch, but reply Yes, I do know, but think it my duty to buy Empire products. Feel at the time, and still think, that this is an excellent reply. Unfortunately Vicky comes into the drawing-room later and says: 'O Mummie, are those the bulbs we got at Woolworths?'

. . . .

Finish the bulbs and put them in the cellar. Feel that after all cellar is probably draughty, change my mind, and take them all up to the attic.

November 13th. – Take a look at bulb-bowls on returning suit-case to attic, and am inclined to think it looks as though the cat had been up here. If so, this will be the last straw. Shall tell Lady Boxe that I sent all my bulbs to a sick friend in a nursing-home.

November 19th. — Consult Cissie about the bulbs, which look very much as if the mice had been at them. She says: Unlimited Watering, and tells me about her own bulbs at Norwich. Am discouraged.

Administer Unlimited Water to the bulbs (some of which goes through the attic floor on to the landing below), and move half of them down to the cellar, as Cissie Crabbe says attic is airless.

December 9th. — On Rose's advice, bring bulb-bowls up from cellar and put them in drawing-room. Several of them perfectly visible, but somehow do not look entirely healthy. Rose thinks too much watering. If so, Cissie Crabbe entirely to blame. (Mem.: Either move bulb-bowls upstairs, or tell Ethel to show Lady Boxe into morning-room, if she calls. Cannot possibly enter into further discussion with her concerning bulbs.)

Xmas Day — Angela looks at bulbs, and says What made me think they would be in flower for Christmas? Do not reply to this.

February 21st. — Remove bulb-bowls, with what is left of bulbs, to greenhouse. Tell Robert that I hope to do better another year. He replies, Another year, better not waste my money.

Loneliness

Trumbull Stickney (1874–1904)

These autumn gardens, russet, gray and brown,
The sward with shrivelled foliage strown,
The shrubs and trees
By weary wings of sunshine overflown
And timid silences, —

Since first you, darling, called my spirit yours,
Seem happy, and the gladness pours
From day to day,
And yester-year across this year endures
Unto next year away.

Now in these places where I used to rove
And give the dropping leaves my love
And weep to them,
They seem to fall divinely from above,
Like to a diadem

Closing in one with the disheartened flowers.
High up the migrant birds in showers
Shine in the sky,
And all the movement of the natural hours
Turns into melody.

Some Observations on Taste

*From Observations on the Theory and Practice of
Landscape Gardening, 1803* | Humphrey Repton (1752–1818)

In every other polite Art, there are certain established rules or
general principles, to which the professor may appeal in support
of his opinions; but in Landscape Gardening every one delivers
his sentiments, or displays his taste, as whim or caprice may
dictate, without having studied the subject, or even thought it
capable of being reduced to any fixed rules. Hence it has been
doubted, whether each proprietor of his own estate, may not be
the most proper person to plan its improvement.

Had the art still continued under the direction of working
gardeners, or nurserymen, the proprietor might supersede the
necessity of such landscape gardeners, provided he had previously
made this art his study; but not, (as it is frequently asserted)
because the gentleman who constantly resides at his place, must
be a better judge of the means of improving it, than the professor
whose visits are only occasional: for if this reason for a preference
were granted, we might with equal truth assert, that the constant
companion of a sick man has an advantage over his physician.

The Best Designer

From *The History of Modern Taste in Gardening, written 1750–1770, published 1780* | Horace Walpole (1717–1797)

In general it is probably true that the possessor, if he has any taste, must be the best designer of his own improvements. He sees his situation in all seasons of the year, at all times of the day. He knows where beauty will not clash with convenience, and observes in his silent walks or accidental rides a thousand hints that must escape a person who in a few days sketches out a pretty picture, but has not had leisure to examine the details and relations of every part.

The Deserted Garden

Verses 1–6 | Elizabeth Barrett Browning (1806–1861)

I mind me in the days departed,
How often underneath the sun
With childish bounds I used to run
    To a garden long deserted.

The beds and walks were vanished quite;
And wheresoe'er had struck the spade,
The greenest grasses Nature laid,
    To sanctify her right.

I called the place my wilderness,
For no one entered there but I;
The sheep looked in, the grass to espy,
    And passed it ne'ertheless.

The trees were interwoven wild,
And spread their boughs enough about
To keep both sheep and shepherd out,
    But not a happy child.

Adventurous joy it was for me!
I crept beneath the boughs, and found
A circle smooth of mossy ground
    Beneath a poplar tree.

Old garden rose-trees hedged it in,
Bedropt with roses waxen-white,
Well satisfied with dew and light,
    And careless to be seen.

Falling Leaves

From *Bleak House, 1852–1853* | Charles Dickens (1812–1870)

CHESNEY WOLD IS SHUT UP:

Around and around the house the leaves fall thick, but never fast,
for they come circling down with a dead lightness that is sombre
and slow. Let the gardener sweep and sweep the turf as he will,
and press the leaves into full barrows, and wheel them off, still
they lie ankle-deep.

12 November

The Vegetable or Kitchen Garden: Forethought

From *The Beeton Book of Garden Management, 1862* | Samuel Orchart Beeton (1831–1877)

Approaching winter bids vegetation prepare for a rest. In the kitchen garden the crops will make little progress for the four months following this. During that time will be apparent the amount of forethought displayed in summer and autumn cropping. If a fair amount of Brussels sprouts, savoys, and other winter vegetables have been provided, this is the main point; and supposing herbs, salading, and minor crops, have been attended to, then, if any ground is unoccupied, lay it up in ridges, having trenched it or dug it deeply, supposing the ground to be light.

Mary, Mary, Quite Contrary

Anon

Mary, Mary, quite contrary,
How does your garden grow?
With silver bells, and cockle shells,
And pretty maids all in a row.

To be done in the Parterre and Flower Garden: Tulips and Protection

From *Kalendarium Hortense, 1664* | John Evelyn (1620–1706)

Now is your best *Season* (the Weather *open*) to, plant your fairest *Tulips* in places of *shelter,* and under *Espaliers;* but let not your *Earth* be too *rich*: *Vide October.*

About the *middle* of this *Month* (or sooner if *Weather* require) quite *enclose* your *tender* Plants, and *perennial Greens, Shrubs,* &c. in your *Conservatory,* secluding all entrance of *Cold,* and especially sharp *Winds.*

Sweep and *cleanse* your *Garden-walks,* and all other places, from *Autumnal* Leaves, the last time.

In the Mood

From *The Well-Tempered Garden, 1970* | Christopher Lloyd
(1921–2006)

As I go about my tasks in the garden it often strikes me that I
am doing this and that at quite the 'wrong' season. I will give a
buddleia a hard prune in the autumn, for instance, or split up and
replant a group of irises in November – at quite the worst time
to be tampering with them. But so often it's a question of now
or never. If you postpone a job until the ideal moment from a
plant's viewpoint, the chances are you will miss doing it when the
moment arrives, for reasons of forgetfulness and preoccupation
with other matters. And so, to the amateur gardener's eternally
repeated question 'when should I' and 'what's the best time to?'
I've concluded that nine times out of ten the answer is 'when
you're thinking about it; when you're in the mood.'

My Garden

Verses 1–4 | Ralph Waldo Emerson (1803–1882)

If I could put my woods in song,
And tell what's there enjoyed,
All men would to my gardens throng,
And leave the cities void.

In my plot no tulips blow,
Snow-loving pines and oaks instead;
And rank the savage maples grow
From spring's faint flush to autumn red.

My garden is a forest ledge
Which older forests bound;
The banks slope down to the blue lake-edge,
Then plunge to depths profound.

Here once the Deluge ploughed,
Laid the terraces, one by one;
Ebbing later whence it flowed,
They bleach and dry in the sun.

The Lewisham Recorder

From *The Story of the Treasure Seekers, 1899* | E. Nesbit
(1858–1924)

18 November

GARDENING NOTES

It is useless to plant cherry stones in the hope of eating the fruit, because they don't!

Alice won't lend her gardening tools again, because the last time Noël left them out in the rain, and I don't like it. He said he didn't.

SEEDS AND BULBS

These are useful to play at shop with, until you are ready. Not at dinner parties, for they will not grow unless uncooked. Potatoes are not grown with seed, but with chopped-up potatoes. Apple trees are grown from twigs, which is less wasteful.

Oak trees come from acorns. Everyone knows this. When Noël says he could grow one from a peach stone wrapped up in oak leaves, he shows that he knows nothing about gardening but marigolds, and when I passed by his garden I thought they seemed just like weeds now the flowers have been picked.

A boy once dared me to eat a bulb.

Dogs are very industrious and fond of gardening. Pincher is always planting bones, but they never grow up. There couldn't be a bone tree. I think this is what makes him bark so unhappily at night. He has never tried planting dog-biscuit, but he is fonder of bones, and perhaps he wants to be quite sure about them first.

The Wrong Weather for Gardening

From *Mary's Meadow* in *Aunt Judy's Magazine, 1883–1884*

Juliana Horatia Ewing (1841–1885)

After the first hard frost we quite gave up playing at the Earthly Paradise; first because there was nothing we could do, and, secondly, because a lot of snow fell, and Arthur had a grand idea of making snow statues all along the terrace, so that Mother could see them from the drawing-room windows. We worked very hard, and it was very difficult to manage legs without breaking; so we made most of them Romans in togas, and they looked very well from a distance, and lasted a long time, because the frost lasted.

The Burning of the Leaves

Laurence Binyon (1869–1943)

Now is the time for the burning of the leaves.
They go to the fire; the nostril pricks with smoke
Wandering slowly into a weeping mist.
Brittle and blotched, ragged and rotten sheaves!
A flame seizes the smouldering ruin and bites
On stubborn stalks that crackle as they resist.

The last hollyhock's fallen tower is dust;
All the spices of June are a bitter reek,
All the extravagant riches spent and mean.
All burns! The reddest rose is a ghost;
Sparks whirl up, to expire in the mist: the wild
Fingers of fire are making corruption clean.

Now is the time for stripping the spirit bare,
Time for the burning of days ended and done,
Idle solace of things that have gone before:
Rootless hopes and fruitless desires are there;
Let them go to the fire, with never a look behind.
The world that was ours is a world that is ours no more.

They will come again, the leaf and the flower, to arise
From squalor of rottenness into the old splendour,
And magical scents to a wondering memory bring;
The same glory, to shine upon different eyes.
Earth cares for her own ruins, naught for ours.
Nothing is certain, only the certain spring.

Topiary Run Wild

From *The Tenant of Wildfell Hall, 1848* | Anne Brontë (1820–1849)

Near the top of this hill, about two miles from Linden-Car, stood
Wildfell Hall, a superannuated mansion of the Elizabethan era,
built of dark grey stone, venerable and picturesque to look at,
but doubtless, cold and gloomy enough to inhabit, with its thick
stone mullions and little latticed panes, its time-eaten air-holes,
and its too lonely, too unsheltered situation, − only shielded from
the war of wind and weather by a group of Scotch firs, themselves
half blighted with storms, and looking as stern and gloomy as
the Hall itself. Behind it lay a few desolate fields, and then the
brown heath-clad summit of the hill; before it (enclosed by
stone walls, and entered by an iron gate, with large balls of grey
granite − similar to those which decorated the roof and gables
− surmounting the gate-posts) was a garden, − once stocked
with such hard plants and flowers as could best brook the soil
and climate, and such trees and shrubs as could best endure the
gardener's torturing shears, and most readily assume the shapes
he chose to give them, − now, having been left so many years
untilled and untrimmed, abandoned to the weeds and the grass,
to the frost and the wind, the rain and the drought, it presented a
very singular appearance indeed. The close green walls of privet,
that had bordered the principal walk, were two-thirds withered
away, and the rest grown beyond all reasonable bounds; the old
boxwood swan, that sat beside the scraper, had lost its neck and
half its body: the castellated towers of laurel in the middle of
the garden, the gigantic warrior that stood on one side of the
gateway, and the lion that guarded the other, were sprouted
into such fantastic shapes as resembled nothing either in heaven
or earth, or in the waters under the earth; but, to my young
imagination, they presented all of them a goblinish appearance,
that harmonised well with the ghostly legions and dark traditions
our old nurse had told us respecting the haunted hall and its
departed occupants.

Hedera

From *The English Flower Garden, 1883* | William Robinson
(1838–1935)

Ivy: *H. helix* is the most beautiful evergreen climber of our northern and temperate world, and is a noble garden plant that may be used in many ways. The common Ivy of the woods is familiar to all, but its many beautiful varieties are not so often seen. All are not of the same vigorous habit, as will easily be seen by cultivating a collection.

. . . .

Ivy as a destroyer: There is hardly an old ruin in England or in N. France that does not bear evidence of Ivy being the most destructive of plants. If put on houses it seeds itself in the most insidious way in places where it is not wanted at all; on walls even. Still, as the most graceful of hardy climbers of the Western world, there must be some place found for it where it cannot ruin; but never on any house, castle, or cottage should it be planted not even on a shed. It grows when we are asleep, and gets its fungus under tiles and walls, and tears off roofs. If we want a climber on the house, there are better things than Ivy as regards flower which will do no harm (Rose Vine and Clematis). There are still many places where Ivy can do no harm, and is very charming on trees I never cut it off trees, rocks and river banks, shelters, bowers in the pleasure garden, when these have strong iron supports, and often as screens on strong trellis-work, pyramids also, and anywhere so long as it is away from any kind of building.

Castle Carabas

From *The Book of Snobs, 1848* | William Makepeace Thackeray
(1811–1863)

A damp green stretch of park spread right and left immeasurably, confined by a chilly grey wall, and a damp long straight road between two huge rows of moist, dismal lime-trees, leads up to the Castle. In the midst of the park is a great black tank or lake, bristling over with rushes, and here and there covered over with patches of pea-soup. A shabby temple rises on an island in this delectable lake, which is approached by a rotten barge that lies at roost in a dilapidated boat house. Clumps of elms and oaks dot over the huge green flat.

Garden Designers

From *The Curious Gardener, 2010* | Anna Pavord (1940–)

Why wouldn't I ever want a real designer swanning around my patch? Let's leave aside the obvious problem of the bill. What I'd resent is the sense of being invaded. My garden is an extension of me, of the things that please me. Forced for most of our lives to operate in a world that is bizarre and irrational (as well as ugly), our gardens become bubbles, protective carapaces. In my garden I can order the world in a way that fits my needs. The ordering, the making of this world, no matter how long it takes, gives one self-esteem (which is not the same thing as vanity or conceit).

'Remember Anna,' a wise gardener said to me. 'A garden is a process, not a product.' In the hands of a garden designer it has little option but to become a product.

This Compost

From *Leaves of Grass, 1867* | Walt Whitman (1819–1892)

1

Something startles me where I thought I was safest,
I withdraw from the still woods I loved,
I will not go now on the pastures to walk,
I will not strip the clothes from my body to meet my lover the sea,
I will not touch my flesh to the earth, as to other flesh to renew
    me.

O how can it be that the ground itself does not sicken?
How can you be alive you growths of spring?
How can you furnish health, you blood of herbs, roots, orchards,
    grain?
Are they not continually putting distemper'd corpses within you?
Is not every continent work'd over and over with sour dead?

Where have you disposed of their carcasses?
Those drunkards and gluttons of so many generations?
Where have you drawn off all the foul liquid and meat?
I do not see any of it upon you to-day, or perhaps I am deceiv'd,
I will run a furrow with my plough, I will press my spade
    through the sod, and turn it up underneath,
I am sure I shall expose some of the foul meat.

2

Behold this compost! behold it well!

Perhaps every mite has once form'd part of a sick person — yet
behold!

The grass of spring covers the prairies,

The bean bursts noiselessly through the mould in the garden,

The delicate spear of the onion pierces upward,

The apple-buds cluster together on the apple-branches,

The resurrection of the wheat appears with pale visage out of its
graves,

The tinge awakes over the willow-tree and the mulberry-tree,

The he-birds carol mornings and evenings while the she-birds sit
on their nests,

The young of poultry break through the hatch'd eggs,

The new-born of animals appear, the calf is dropt from the cow,
the colt from the mare,

Out of its little hill faithfully rise the potato's dark green leaves,

Out of its hill rises the yellow maize-stalk, the lilacs bloom in the
dooryards,

The summer growth is innocent and disdainful above all those
strata of sour dead.

What chemistry!

That the winds are really not infectious,

That this is no cheat, this transparent green-wash of the sea, which is so amorous after me,

That it is safe to allow it to lick my naked body all over with its
   tongues,

That it will not endanger me with the fevers that have deposited
   themselves in it,

That all is clean forever and forever,

That the cool drink from the well tastes so good,

That blackberries are so flavorous and juicy,

That the fruits of the apple-orchard, and the orange-orchard −
   that melons, grapes, peaches, plums, will none of them poison
   me,

That when I recline on the grass I do not catch any disease,

Though probably every spear of grass rises out of what was once a
   catching disease.

Now I am terrified at the earth, it is that calm and patient,

It grows such sweet things out of such corruptions,

It turns harmless and stainless on its axis, with such endless
   successions of diseas'd corpses,

It distills such exquisite winds out of such infused fetor,

It renews with such unwitting looks, its prodigal, annual,
   sumptuous crops,

It gives such divine materials to men, and accepts such leavings
   from them at last.

Houseplants

From *Instructions in Gardening for Ladies, 1840* | Jane Loudon
(1807–1858)

The management of plants in rooms is extremely difficult from
the want of proper light and pure air: though this latter want may,
in some measure, be obviated, by opening the window in front
of which the plants stand, whenever circumstances will permit.
It should never be forgotten that fresh air is almost as essential to
plants as water; and that they are seriously injured by being forced
to inspire air at their breathing pores that is in an unfit state for
them. I have often observed the healthy appearance of plants
belonging to cottagers; and I believe it arises principally from the
habit that most poor people have, of setting their plants out in the
rain whenever there is a shower. This not only clears the leaves
of dust, and opens the stomata, or breathing, pores, but gives
the plant abundance of fresh air. Without a sufficiency of air and
light, plants will soon become weak and sickly, and their leaves
will turn yellow; but if a little fresh air be given to them every
day when the temperature is not too cold, they will grow quite as
well in a room as in a green-house.

The Man Kent

From *Old Country Life, 1890* | Rev. Sabine Baring-Gould (1834–1924)

The man Kent deserved the gallows much more than many
who have been hung. No one who pretended to be in fashion
dared to maintain a hedge or a wall. Down went the walls, and
the beautiful roses bent their heads and died; the great yew
hedges were stubbed up, and the delicate children and feeble
old gentlemen who had basked under the lea, also, like the
roses, stooped to earth and died. All the shelter, sweetness, sun,
restfulness went away. These hedges had taken a century or more
to grow, they were levelled without compunction, never perhaps
again to reappear.

27 November

The Gardens of Alcinoüs

From *Odyssey, Book VII, translated by Alexander Pope, 1715–1720* | Homer (12/8th century BC) | Translated by Alexander Pope (1688–1744)

Close to the gates a spacious garden lies,
From storms defended and inclement skies.
Four acres was the allotted space of ground,
Fenced with a green enclosure all around.
Tall thriving trees confess'd the fruitful mould:
The reddening apple ripens here to gold.
Here the blue fig with luscious juice o'erflows,
With deeper red the full pomegranate glows;
The branch here bends beneath the weighty pear,
And verdant olives flourish round the year,
The balmy spirit of the western gale
Eternal breathes on fruits, unthought to fail:
Each dropping pear a following pear supplies,
On apples apples, figs on figs arise:
The same mild season gives the blooms to blow,
The buds to harden, and the fruits to grow.

Here order'd vines in equal ranks appear,
With all the united labours of the year;

Some to unload the fertile branches run,
Some dry the blackening clusters in the sun,
Others to tread the liquid harvest join:
The groaning presses foam with floods of wine
Here are the vines in early flower descried,
Here grapes discolour'd on the sunnyside,
And there in autumn's richest purple dyed,
    Beds of all various herbs, for ever green,
In beauteous order terminate the scene.
    Two plenteous fountains the whole prospect crown'd
This through the gardens leads its streams around
Visits each plant, and waters all the ground;
While that in pipes beneath the palace flows,
And thence its current on the town bestows:
To various use their various streams they bring,
The people one, and one supplies the king.
    Such were the glories which the gods ordain'd,
To grace Alcinoüs, and his happy land.

An Abrupt Change

From *Cuttings from My Garden Notebooks, 1997* | Graham Stuart
Thomas (1909–2003)

After a night of storm towards the end of November, sometimes
it happens that one awakes to a garden transformed. The best
tinted leaves have fallen and all have been driven into corners off
the paths and lawns, revealing the fresh green of the grass and
the contrast of paving and gravel. The leaves are off the trees,
giving more light to the garden, and the spectral shadows of bare
branches steal across the lawn. The old year has gone, all its glory,
its successes and failures, and we are abruptly brought to face
winter, with berries and leaves almost alone as colour-givers.

29 November

Autumn

From *The Woodlanders, 1887* | Thomas Hardy (1840–1928)

Autumn drew shiveringly to its end. One day something seemed
to be gone from the gardens; the tenderer leaves of vegetables
had shrunk under the first smart frost, and hung like faded
linen rags; then the forest leaves, which had been descending at
leisure, descended in haste and in multitudes, and all the golden
colours that had hung overhead were now crowded together in
a degraded mass underfoot, where the fallen myriads got redder
and hornier, and curled themselves up to rot.

DECEMBER

The Genius of the Place

Domicilium

Thomas Hardy (1840–1928)

It faces west, and round the back and sides
High beeches, bending, hang a veil of boughs,
And sweep against the roof. Wild honeysucks
Climb on the walls, and seem to sprout a wish
(If we may fancy wish of trees and plants)
To overtop the apple-trees hard by.

Red roses, lilacs, variegated box
Are there in plenty, and such hardy flowers
As flourish best untrained. Adjoining these
Are herbs and esculents; and farther still
A field; then cottages with trees, and last
The distant hills and sky.

Behind, the scene is wilder. Heath and furze
Are everything that seems to grow and thrive
Upon uneven ground. A stunted thorn
Stands here and there, indeed; and from a pit
An oak uprises, springing from a seed
Dropped by some bird a hundred years ago.

In days bygone –
Long gone – my father's mother, who is now
Blest with the blest, would take me out to walk.
At such a time I once inquired of her
How looked the spot when she first settled here.
The answer I remember. 'Fifty years
Have passed since then, my child, and change has marked
The face of all things. Yonder garden-plots
And orchards were uncultivated slopes
O'ergrown with bramble bushes, furze and thorn:
That road a narrow path shut in by ferns,
Which, almost trees, obscured the passer-by.

Our house stood quite alone, and those tall firs
And beeches were not planted. Snakes and efts
Swarmed in the summer days, and nightly bats
Would fly about our bedrooms. Heathcroppers
Lived on the hills, and were our only friends;
So wild it was when we first settled here.'

The Rules for an Ideal Rockery

From *My Rock Garden, 1907* | Reginald Farrer (1880–1920)

Briefly, there is but one. Have an idea, and stick to it. Let
your rock-garden set out to be something definite, not a mere
agglomeration of stones. Let it be a mountain gorge, if you
like, or the stony slope of a hill, or a rocky crest, or a peak.
But, whatever it be, it must have definiteness of scheme. It is, in
effect, an imitation of Nature, and, to be successful, must aim
at reproducing with fidelity some particular feature of Nature –
whichever you may choose.

A Word of Warning

From *My Garden, 1971* | H. E. Bates (1905–1974)

If you have a bare or ugly space to cover do not be tempted to plant
the Russian Vine *Polygonatum baldschuanicum;* you will for ever live
to regret acquaintance with this possessive, unbeautiful octopus.
Rapidity of growth may be a virtue, but it isn't everything.

3 December

The Garden at Planes

From *The Pursuit of Love, 1945* | Nancy Mitford (1904–1973)

The garden which lay around it would be a lady water-colourist's
heaven, herbaceous borders, rockeries, and water-gardens were
carried to a perfection of vulgarity, and flaunted a riot of huge
and hideous flowers, each individual bloom appearing twice
as large, three times as brilliant as it ought to have been and if
possible of a different colour from that which nature intended.
It would be hard to say whether it was more frightful, more like
glorious Technicolor, in spring, in summer, or in autumn. Only
in the depth of winter, covered by kindly snow, did it melt into
the landscape and become tolerable.

Decembers Husbandrie

From *Five Hundred Points of Good Husbandry, 1557, 1573*

Thomas Tusser (1524–1580)

Strawberies.

If frost doe continue, take this for a lawe,
    the strawberies looke to be covered with strawe.
Laid overly trim upon crotchis and bows,
    and after uncovered as weather allows.

Gille Flowers.

The gilleflower also, the skilful doe knowe,
    doe looke to be covered, in frost and in snowe.
The knot, and the border, and rosemarie gaie,
    do crave the like succour for dieng awaie.

The Mediterranean Garden

From *Garden Notebook, 1988* | Beth Chatto (1923–2018)

On a crisp, sunny morning I walk out of my back door into the little Mediterranean garden and see good foliage all around me. Although we are at the lowest ebb of the year, there is almost total ground cover in this part of the garden. The sky is blue; the colour and texture of every leaf stands out clearly. The main spires of the borders are made with Rosemary, Lavender, *Cistus* and *Phlomis fruticosa*. A sea-green shrub of *Bupleurum fruticosum* is still covered with umbellifer-like seed heads. Beside it a blue-leafed cypress which we bought as *Cupressus arizonica,* but which might be a form of *Cupressus glabra,* dominates this border while nearer the house *Libocedrus decurrens,* like a dark green totem pole, towers above the roof line.

To be done in the Parterre and Flower Garden: Vermine and Frosts

From *Kalendarium Hortense, 1664* | John Evelyn (1620–1706)

As in *January,* continue your *hostility* against *Vermine.*

Preserve from too much *Rain* and *Frost* your choicest *Anemones, Ranunculus's, Carnations,* &c.

Be careful now to keep the *Doors* and *Windows* of your *Conservatories* well *matted* and guarded from the piercing Air; for your *Oranges,* &c. are now put to the *test.*

Look to your *Fountain-Pipes,* and cover them with fresh and *warm Litter* out of the *Stable,* a good *thickness,* lest the *Frosts* crack them; remember it in *time,* and the *Advice* will save you both Trouble and Charge.

Mrs Beattie's Parties

From *The Real Charlotte, 1894* | Somerville & Ross

E. Œ. / Edith Somerville (1858–1949) & Martin Ross / Violet Florence Martin (1862–1915)

Mrs Beattie gave but two parties in the year – one at Christmas, on account of the mistletoe; and one in July, on account of the raspberries, for which her garden was justly famous.

The Garden

1861 | Andrew Marvell (1621–1678)

VERSES 1 AND 2

i

How vainly men themselves amaze
To win the Palm, the Oke or Bayes,
And their uncessant Labours see
Crown'd from some single Herb or Tree,
Whose short and narrow verged Shade
Does prudently their Toyles upbraid,
While all Flow'rs and all Trees do close
To weave the Garlands of repose.

ii

Fair quiet, have I found thee here,
And Innocence, thy Sister dear!
Mistaken long, I sought you then
In busie Companies of Men.
Your sacred Plants, if here below,
Only among the Plants will grow.
Society is all but rude,
To this delicious Solitude.

The Pleasures of Fruit-Trees

From *A Treatise of Fruit Trees, 1653* | Ralph Austen (c.1612–1676)

First to the Eare, and in that two respects, first by sweete tunes of singing birds, secondly by gentle motion of Boughes, and leaves.

Secondly, Here's Pleasure to the Touch, and that in two respects, first, by coole fruits, Boughes and Leaves: secondly by coole fresh Aires.

Thirdly, Here's Pleasure to the Eye, and that in two respects, first by exact and decent forms of Trees, Alleyes, Walkes, Seates, and Arbours: secondly, by curious colours of the blossomes, Leaves, and fruits.

Here's Pleasure to the smell, and that in two respects: first, from fresh Earth digged up: secondly, from the Leaves, and Blossoms.

Fifthly, Here's Pleasure to the tast, and that in two respects: first from ripe, and raw fruits, Secondly, from dishes and drinkes made of them.

Shrubberies

From *Orlando, 1928* | Virginia Woolf (1882–1941)

Stealthily and imperceptibly, none marking the exact day or hour of the change, the constitution of England was altered and nobody knew it. Everywhere the effects were felt.

. . . .

No garden, however formal its original design, lacked a shrubbery, a wilderness, a maze.

. . . .

Eusebius Chubb screwed the lid of his inkpot and went for a turn in his garden. Soon he found himself involved in the shrubbery. Innumerable leaves creaked and glistened above his head. He seemed to himself 'to crush the mould of a million more under his feet'. Thick smoke exuded from a damp bonfire at the end of the garden. He reflected that no fire on earth could ever hope to consume that vast vegetable encumbrance. Wherever he looked, vegetation was rampant. Cucumbers 'came scrolloping across the grass to his feet'. Giant cauliflowers towered deck above deck till they rivalled, to his disordered imagination, the elm trees themselves.

The Impossibility of Shrubberies

From *The English Gardener, 1829* | William Cobbett (1763–1835)

Shrubberies should be so planted, if they be of any considerable depth, as for the tallest trees to be at the back, and the lowest in front; if one could have one's will, one would go, by slow degrees, from a dwarf Kalmia to a Catalpa or Horse-chestnut. Such a slope, however, would require the depth of a mile; and, therefore, is out of the question.

The Genius of the Place

From *Moral Essays, 1731–1753* | Alexander Pope (1688–1744)
Epistle IV to Richard Boyle, Earl of Burlington, lines 57–64

Consult the Genius of the Place in all;
That tells the Waters or to rise, or fall,
Or helps th' ambitious Hill the heav'ns to scale,
Or scoops in circling theatres the Vale;
Calls in the Country, catches op'ning glades,
Joins willing woods, and varies shades from shades;
Now breaks, or now directs, th' intending Lines,
Paints as you plant, and, as you work, designs.

The Importance of Unexpectedness

From *Headlong Hall, 1816* | Thomas Love Peacock (1785–1866)

'Allow me,' said Mr Gall. 'I distinguish the picturesque and the beautiful, and I add to them, in the laying out of grounds, a third and distinct character, which I call *unexpectedness*.'

'Pray, sir,' said Mr Milestone, 'by what name do you distinguish this character, when a person walks round the grounds for the second time?

Mr Gall bit his lips, and inwardly vowed to revenge himself on Milestone, by cutting up his next publication.

Mole End

From *The Wind in the Willows, 1908* | Kenneth Grahame (1859–1932)

Mole reached down a lantern from a nail on the wall and lit it, and the Rat, looking round him, saw that they were in a sort of fore-court. A garden-seat stood on one side of the door, and on the other a roller; for the Mole, who was a tidy animal when at home, could not stand having his ground kicked up by other animals into little runs that ended in earth-heaps. On the walls hung wire baskets with ferns in them, alternating with brackets carrying plaster statuary – Garibaldi, and the infant Samuel, and Queen Victoria, and other heroes of modern Italy. Down on one side of the fore-court ran a skittle-alley, with benches along it and little wooden tables marked with rings that hinted at beer-mugs. In the middle was a small round pond containing goldfish and surrounded by a cockle-shell border. Out of the centre of the pond rose a fanciful erection clothed in more cockle-shells and topped by a large silvered glass ball that reflected everything all wrong and had a very pleasing effect.

The Needs of Plants

From *Natural Planting, 1997* | Penelope Hobhouse (1929–)

It is infinitely complicated, but infinitely fascinating, to discover what plants need to grow – both in the wild and when moved into a garden. Plants respond to conditions offered locally by the changing seasons that enable them to make growth and to flower at the appropriate times. Given adequate supplies of light, moisture and nutrients, the main factors controlling the growth of a plant (and consequently its selection for the garden) are hardiness and appropriate soil. The gardener does not need to know the detailed physiological changes that take place in plants, but a basic idea of what is going on not only has thoroughly practical advantages (like preventing you from losing a moisture-lover by planting it in a dry spot, and from wasting effort on plants that cannot tolerate temperature where you live), but also enriches gardeners' appreciation of the plants they grow – especially those that come originally from halfway round the globe.

Knowing where a plant comes from is the first step in the natural gardening process. Not just the country, but the terrain that provides its local habitat. The natural approach simply means trying to provide the plant with a habitat as close as possible to its original home and surrounding it with plants with similar needs. Probably coming from similar habitats in different regions of the world.

Gardeners are always working in this way – so frequently that we are unaware of doing so.

Definition and Pronunciation

From *Dictionary of the English Language, 1755* | Samuel Johnson
(1709–1784) | John Walker (1732–1807)

GARDEN:

A piece of ground, enclosed and cultivated with extraordinary
care, planted with herbs or fruits for food, or laid out for pleasure.

IN 1805 THE DICTIONARY WAS PUBLISHED WITH PRONUNCIATION
NOTES FROM *WALKER'S PRONOUNCING DICTIONARY:*

When the a, in this and similar words, is preceded by g or k,
polite speakers interpose a sound like the consonant y, which
coalesces with both, and gives a mellowness to the sound: thus, a
garden, pronounced in this manner, is nearly similar to the two
words egg and yarden united into eggyarden.

17 December

Green Groweth the Holly

King Henry VIII (1491–1547)

Green groweth the holly,
So doth the ivy.
Though winter blasts blow never so high,
Green groweth the holly.

As the holly groweth green
And never changeth hue,
So I am, ever hath been,
Unto my lady true.

As the holly groweth green
With ivy all alone
When flowers cannot be seen
And greenwood leaves be gone,

Now unto my lady
Promise to her I make,
From all other only
To her I me betake.

Adieu, mine own lady,
Adieu, my special
Who hath my heart truly
Be sure, and ever shall.

Talking to the Lilies on the Moon

From *Doctor Dolittle in the Moon, 1928* | Hugh Lofting (1886–1947)

The Doctor – 'Do you like this stationary life – I mean, living in the same place all the time, unable to move?'

The Lilies – (Several of them seemed to answer in chorus) – 'Why, yes – of course. Being stationary doesn't bother us. We hear about all that is going on.'

The Doctor – 'From whom, what, do you hear it?'

The Lilies – 'Well, the other plants, the bees, the birds, bring us news of what is happening.'

The Doctor – 'Oh, do you communicate with the bees and the birds?'

The Lilies – 'Why, certainly, of course!'

The Doctor – 'Yet the bees and the birds are races different from your own.'

The Lilies – 'Quite true, but the bees come to us for honey. And the birds come to sit among our leaves – especially the warblers – and they sing and talk and tell us of what is happening in the world. What more would you want?'

The Doctor – 'Oh, quite so, quite so. I didn't mean you should be discontented. But don't you ever want to move, to travel?'

The Lilies – 'Good gracious, no! What's the use of all this running about? After all, there's no place like home – provided it's a good one. It's a pleasant life we lead – and very safe. The folks who rush around are always having accidents, breaking legs and so forth. Those troubles can't happen to us. We sit still and watch the world go by. We chat sometimes among ourselves and then there is always the gossip of the birds and the bees to entertain us.'

The Doctor – 'And you really understand the language of the birds and bees! – You astonish me.'

The Lilies – 'Oh, perfectly – and of the beetles and moths too.'

Moon Plants

From *The First Men in the Moon, 1901* | H. G. Wells (1866–1946)

Amidst the stick-like litter were these rounded bodies, these little oval bodies that might have passed as very small pebbles. And now first one and then another had stirred, had rolled over and cracked, and down the crack of each of them showed a minute line of yellowish green, thrusting outward to meet the hot encouragement of the newly-risen sun. For a moment that was all, and then there stirred, and burst a third!

. . . .

Every moment more of these seed coats ruptured, and even as they did so the swelling pioneers overflowed their rent-distended seed-cases, and passed into the second stage of growth. With a steady assurance, a swift deliberation, these amazing seeds thrust a rootlet downward to the earth and a queer little bundle-like bud into the air. In a little while the whole slope was dotted with minute plantlets standing at attention in the blaze of the sun. They did not stand for long. The bundle-like buds swelled and strained and opened with a jerk, thrusting out a coronet of little sharp tips, spreading a whorl of tiny, spiky, brownish leaves, that lengthened rapidly, lengthened visibly even as we watched. The movement was slower than any animal's, swifter than any plant's I have ever seen before. How can I suggest it to you — the way that growth went on? The leaf tips grew so that they moved onward even while we looked at them. The brown seed-case shrivelled and was absorbed with an equal rapidity. Have you ever on a cold day taken a thermometer into your warm hand and watched the little thread of mercury creep up the tube? These moon plants grew like that.

Mature yet Changing

From *The Ivington Diaries, 2009* | Monty Don (1955–)

One of the great virtues of a garden is that it is so temporal
and human in scale. A garden seven years old can seem mature
and after fifteen years few would be able to date it closer than
a decade. I recall visiting the oldest garden in Britain, Levens
Hall in Cumbria, made in the 1690s and famous for its huge
and Baroque topiary, and idly asking how long it would take to
recreate the garden should it be bulldozed? Thirty years. That is
all. Everything after that would simply be holding it in check.

The truth is that a mature garden is surprisingly short-term and
attainable. For the first three years it is all dreams and schemes.
For the next four there is the satisfaction of seeing it come into
being, the next seven a gradual maturation and after that it is a
rhythm of maintenance and curtailment.

. . . .

The idea that you can fix any part of a garden in time or even in
place is doomed to fail. Nothing stays exactly as you want it to
and nothing is ever finished. That is the beauty of making
a garden.

Duty or Pleasure?

From *Elizabeth and her German Garden, 1898* | Elizabeth Von Arnim (1866–1941)

I am very busy preparing for Christmas, but have often locked myself up in a room alone, shutting out my unfinished duties, to study the flower catalogues and make my lists of seeds and shrubs and trees for the spring. It is a fascinating occupation, and acquires an additional charm when you know you ought to be doing something else, that Christmas is at the door, that children and servants and farm hands depend on you for their pleasure, and that, if you don't see to the decoration of the trees and house, and the buying of the presents, nobody else will. The hours fly by shut up with those catalogues and with Duty snarling on the other side of the door. I don't like Duty – everything in the least disagreeable is always sure to be one's duty. Why cannot it be my duty to make lists and plans for the dear garden? 'And so it is,' I insisted to the Man of Wrath, when he protested against what he called wasting my time upstairs. 'No,' he replied sagely; 'your garden is not your Duty, because it is your Pleasure.'

Grass Paths

From *The Trumpet-Major, 1880* | Thomas Hardy (1840–1928)

This garden was undivided from Loveday's, the two having
originally been the single garden of the whole house. It was a
quaint old place, enclosed by a thorn hedge so shapely and dense
from incessant clipping that the mill-boy could walk along the
top without sinking in — a feat which he often performed as a
means of filling out his day's work. The soil within was of that
intense fat blackness which is only seen after a century of constant
cultivation. The paths were grassed over, so that people came and
went upon them without being heard. The grass harboured slugs,
and on this account the miller was going to replace it by gravel
as soon as he had time; but as he had said this for thirty years
without doing it, the grass and the slugs seemed likely to remain.

Quince Trees

From *Better Gardening, 1982* | Robin Lane Fox (1946–)

The home of the quince is Central Asia, as harsh a climate as
anything in British gardens. It soon reached the Aegean, because
early Greek poets already use the quince as a simile for the
silky skin of a girl. The fruits and their points are compared
with her other attributes. At the other end of the globe, quinces
were probably the famous Golden Peaches of Samarkand which
travelled with traders north-east from the river Oxus through the
intervening deserts of the Silk Road to the centres of seventh-
century Tang China. There is a story, later, that the Chinese bred
their own 'golden peaches' by grafting a peach and a persimmon,
but I do not think this refers to the original 'Golden Peach'. I
like to think of its first arrival from Central Asia in the exquisite
circles of Tang China, where it would have accompanied the
dances and new music, furs, jewellery and radical religions which
burst on Chinese society from their source in the distant West.
Away beyond the White Dragon Dunes and the Mountains of
Heaven lay the home of Golden Peaches. The thought sustains
one's interest in a quince-tree even when it has lost its leaves.

The Harmonious Tree

From *Tales from the Arabian Nights' Entertainments, first English translation 1704–1717* | Translated by Rev. George Fyler Townsend (1814–1900)

THE STORY OF THE THREE SISTERS: THE EMPEROR ASKS TO SEE THE GARDENS:

25 December

The princess opened a door which led into the garden, and conducted him to the spot where the harmonious-tree was planted and there the emperor heard a concert, different from all he had ever heard before; and stopping to see where the musicians were, he could discern nobody far or near, but still distinctly heard the music, which ravished his senses. 'My daughter,' said he to the princess, 'where are the musicians whom I hear? Are they underground, or invisible in the air? Such excellent performers will lose nothing by being seen; on the contrary, they would please the more.'

'Sire,' answered the princess, smiling, 'they are not musicians, but the leaves of the tree your majesty sees before you, which form this concert; and if you will give yourself the trouble to go a little nearer, you will be convinced, for the voices will be the more distinct.'

The emperor went nearer, and was so charmed with the sweet harmony, that he could never have been tired with hearing it.

Kubla Khan

1816 | Samuel Taylor Coleridge (1772–1834)

LINES 1–11

In Xanadu did Kubla Khan
A stately pleasure-dome decree:
Where Alph, the sacred river, ran
Through caverns measureless to man
     Down to a sunless sea.
So twice five miles of fertile ground
With walls and towers were girdled round:
And there were gardens bright with sinuous rills,
Where blossomed many an incense-bearing tree;
And here were forests as ancient as the hills,
Enfolding sunny spots of greenery.

Labels

From *Gardening for Beginners, 1901* | E. T. Cook (1867–1915)

Everything sown or planted in a garden should be labelled, such as all varieties of Apples or other fruits, of Dahlias, Roses, Carnations, and other things individually, and Peas, Potatoes, Cabbages, &c., in the bulk. Labels may be made easily from stout laths rent for plastering, as these need little preparation. A bundle of laths 3 feet long will make hundreds of labels, from 4 inches, wired on to trees or roses, up to 8 inches, for vegetables. First cut them into proper lengths, then pointed one end, if to be put in the ground, doing that with a sharp knife, and facing off both sides flatwise quite smooth. A little thin white paint may be well rubbed over a few inches of the top of one side, and the name be written with pencil whilst the paint is wet. It then soon dries, and the writing will remain clear as long as the label endures. These wood labels should be prepared by the fireside in the winter.

27 December

Pleasures in Winter

From *The Well-Tempered Garden, 1970* | Christopher Lloyd
(1921–2006)

We hear and read a lot about the garden in winter but, speaking
for myself, it gives me little actual pleasure. Nearly all pleasurable
thoughts are in looking forward, in noting bulbs pushing
through, the number of dormant flower buds on shrubs and trees
and so on.

The Guinea-Pigs' Garden

From *Cecily Parsley's Nursery Rhymes, 1922* | Beatrix Potter
(1866–1943)

We have a little garden,
    A garden of our own,
And every day we water there
    The seeds that we have sown.

We love our little garden,
    And tend it with such care,
You will not find a faded leaf
    Or blighted blossom there.

The Vegetable or Kitchen Garden: Seeds and Litter

From *The Beeton Book of Garden Management, 1862* | Samuel Orchart Beeton (1831–1877)

Seeds: Some attention should be given, both to the various stores of seeds and vegetables; the latter should be looked over occasionally, turned, sorted, and cleaned; kept moist without being damp, cool without frost, and where there is a free circulation of air. As to seeds, it is well to have them ready for sowing; that is, thoroughly dried and rubbed out, every particle of husk and light seed blown out, and carefully papered and labelled.

Those that have to be purchased should be procured early. Go to respectable dealers, who can be certain of the sorts being true to name. Note down and procure exactly what will be required for the season, so that no time is lost in running after them the moment they are wanted, and place each sort in its proper drawer or receptacle, that there may be no confusion.

Removal of Litter: Nothing, perhaps, is more objectionable, even in the winter months than an untidy garden. Leaves and all litter of dead and dying plants should be collected and carried away, and neatness and order should be everywhere apparent.

New Year's Eve

David Austin (1926–2018)

The leaves have gone from the trees.
The plants rest in the warm earth.
The trees wait, tall and bare
the wind in their upper branches,
while beneath, all is still and quiet.

There is a peace in this lack of life,
like the stillness of a silent god.
There is no struggle,
life rests,
I will wait here
while my mind unwinds
the trauma of a torn year.

Index

Acknowledgements

John Agard, *Talking to Plants* with permission of Bloodaxe Books.

H. E. Bates, *A Love of Flowers*, Curtis Brown Group Ltd, London on behalf of the Estate of H. E. Bates. Copyright © H. E. Bates, 1971.

E. F. Benson, *Mapp and Lucia*, © E. F. Benson, Heinemann.

E. F. Benson, *Queen Lucia*, © E. F. Benson, Heinemann.

E. A. Bowles, *My Garden in Summer*, © E. A. Bowles, David & Charles Ltd.

Extracts from GARDEN NOTEBOOK By Beth Chatto, © Beth Chatto 1988. Reproduced by permission of Sheil Land Associates Ltd.

Walter de la Mare, *Two Gardens*. Courtesy of The Literary Trustees of Walter de la Mare and the Society of Authors as their Representative.

Monty Don, *The Ivington Diaries*, © Monty Don, 2009, *The Ivington Diaries*, Bloomsbury Publishing Plc.

The Jewel Garden by Monty and Sarah Don © 2004, Monty and Sarah Don. Reproduced by permission of Hodder & Stoughton.

Daphne du Maurier, *Rebecca*, © The Estate of Daphne du Maurier. Curtis Brown Group Ltd, London.

Margery Fish, *Cottage Garden Flowers*, © Margery Fish, by permission of B. T. Batsford Ltd.

Margery Fish, *We Made a Garden*, © Margery Fish, by permission of B. T. Batsford Ltd.

Leon Garfield, *The Pleasure Garden*, © Leon Garfield, Penguin Random House.

David Hicks, *Cotswold Gardens*, © David Hicks, Orion Publishing Group.

Penelope Hobhouse, *Natural Planting*, © Penelope Hobhouse, Pavilion Books.

From *Modern Nature* by Derek Jarman published by Century. Copyright © Derek Jarman 1991. Reprinted by permission of The Random House Group Limited.

Robin Lane Fox, *Better Gardening*, © Robin Lane, InkWell Management Literary Agency.

'Sunlight on the Garden' from *Collected Poems* by Louis MacNeice (Faber & Faber), reproduced by permission of David Higham Associates.

Nancy Mitford, *Love from Nancy*, © Nancy Mitford, Hodder & Stoughton.

Nancy Mitford, *The Pursuit of Love*, © Nancy Mitford, Penguin Random House.

Beverley Nichols, *Down the Garden Path*, © Beverley Nichols, Jonathan Cape, Penguin Random House.

Mirabel Osler, *In the Eye of the Garden*, © Mirabel Osler, Orion Publishing Group.

Russell Page, *The Education of a Gardener*, © Russell Page, Harvill Secker, Penguin Random House.

Anna Pavord, *The Curious Gardener*, © Anna Pavord, 2011, *The*